Strategic Church Administration

Managing the Work of the Kingdom

By

Dr. Stan DeKoven

Vision Publishing

1115 D Street

Ramona, CA 92065

(760) 789-4700

www.visionpublishingservices.com

All scripture references taken from the New American Standard Version.

ISBN 1-931178-64-X

Table of Contents

INTRODUCTION

For many students of ministry, along with pastors, etc., administration has become a "dirty word." Most of us would like to devote ourselves to prayer and the ministry of the Word (Acts 6:1-6) exclusively. Yet, church ministry requires administrative skills and capabilities. Without them, as the Apostles found in the passage referred to, the church cannot fully function.

Some of the material for this book was adopted from teaching notes by David S. Land, (Church Business and Office Management). The author is grateful for permission to adopt this material.

You will note that there is provided here a model for incorporation of your ministry. It is provided for general information, not specific implementation. It is strongly recommended that, if you need assistance in incorporation, that you contact a qualified ministry consultant.

Church management and administration must flow from a biblical model and understanding of church government. Government flows from Christ as head of the church; through the Holy Spirit, the administrator of the church through gifts/offices/five-fold ministry; through elders/deacons and the ministry of all believers (every joint supplying). These concepts are key to our understanding of Strategic Church Administration.

I trust as you read this material that it will assist you in developing the mind of Christ, to advance the work God has called you to.

ACKNOWLEDGEMENTS

The writing of this book has been, for all intents and purposes, an administrative chore, a necessary task to be completed. I'm glad it is done! Writing this required significant help, for which I am grateful, and includes the following key people:

- Rebecca Volosin, my daughter and assistant on this writing project.
- Mr. Richard Nissen (S.P.), who is by far the finest technical editor in the business.
- Don Buckel, Director of Administrative Assistance, who reviewed this work, making many comments which were helpful and challenging.
- The staff of Vision International for their willingness to help as required.

"The elders who rule well are to be considered worthy of double honor, especially those who work hard at preaching and teaching. For the Scripture says, "YOU SHALL NOT MUZZLE THE OX WHILE HE IS THRESHING," and "The laborer is worthy of his wages."
1 Timothy 5:17-18

CHAPTER 1

ELDERS AND DEACONS: PURPOSE, PERSONALITY, POTENTIAL

Purpose: Eldership In Israel

Our God is a God of purpose and pattern. The author of Hebrews tells us that these things were a "shadow of things to come" (Heb. 10:1). The pattern for the priesthood in the old covenant reflects the New Testament priesthood of the believer, and the Tabernacle reflects the progressive work of salvation that begins at the brazen altar, Calvary, where Christ Himself was offered once and for all. In the same manner, we see a pattern for New Testament church government in the Eldership of Israel, beginning with the primary purpose of leading and caring for the people of God.

Let me digress for a moment, and discuss the biblical principle of primary purpose. The primary purpose of the cross is to deliver people from sin to serve the Savior. With redemption a reality, we enjoy the secondary purposes of healing, prosperity, and peace. You can go to heaven sick, poor and without peace, but you cannot go to heaven without Jesus. By understanding the principle of primary and secondary purposes, we can "rightly divide the word" of God and set our priorities in line with the priorities of God.

When Israel was delivered out of Egypt, it was a theocratic nation governed by God through His man Moses. It is significant that the name Moses means "drawer out." In this we see the primary purpose of the Fivefold Ministry - to draw out a people for God, to draw out the gifting that God has placed in individuals' lives.

> Ephesians 4:8, "...He led captivity captive and He gave gifts to men", 11, "...And He gave some Apostles, and some Prophets, and some Evangelists, and some Pastors, Teachers", 12, "...For the perfecting of the saints for the work of the ministry for the edifying of the body of Christ."

There is a specific order given to the Fivefold Ministry found in I Corinthians 12:27 - "And God set some in the church, first Apostles, second Prophets, third Teachers (Pastor/Teachers), after that miracles, helps, governments, diversity of tongues." This order is purposeful, not accidental. Apostles and prophets lay a purposeful, God-ordained foundation for ministry. Teachers, and pastors, and other ministries are to build on the foundation. Christ, himself, is the cornerstone of this spiritual building called the church. In modern times, most ministries are built on pastoral or other foundations, with pastoral-led (one man or woman) local congregational government, an adaptation foreign to New Testament teaching. More on these principles later; now back to Moses.

Moses drew the children of Israel out of Egypt, leading them toward the promised land. A pillar of cloud overshadowed them by day, turning to a pillar of fire by night.

Covered by God, the new nation had a caring leader who soon discovered his own limitations. Moses was wearing out!

Can you imagine the care of almost three million people? A city of three million has thousands, perhaps tens of thousands of city workers, headed by a mayor, or a city council. The judicial system has lower and higher courts, justices, and a chief justice. Moses in essence was being all of these and more to Israel. Only the intervention of his father-in-law Jethro saved Moses and Israel from complete disaster. Jethro had a better idea. In fact, as seen in the book *Leadership and Vision*, it was a better plan, but perhaps not God's best. This will be more clearly presented soon.

> Exodus 18:21-23 - *"Furthermore, you shall select out of all the people able men who fear God, men of truth, those who hate dishonest gain; and you shall place these over them, as leaders of thousands, of hundreds, of fifties and of tens. 22 And let them judge the people at all times; and let it be that every major dispute they will bring to you, but every minor dispute they themselves will judge. So it will be easier for you, and they will bear the burden with you. 23 If you do this thing and God so commands you, then you will be able to endure, and all these people also will go to their place in peace."*

The Elders of Israel were not chosen to serve the people. They were chosen to serve Moses. The primary principle of Eldership is this:

> Eldership serves the Fivefold Ministry gift(s) that leads the local church, as the Fivefold Ministry serves as the hand of Christ extended over His church in the locality.

Without a clear understanding of this principle, there will always be confusion concerning the role of an Elder in the church,[1] which ultimately results in a lack of leadership or a power struggle among the leadership, two things that no church can afford. Let's look to the pattern to see the primary purpose of Eldership, even though the pattern was not adequately followed by the leaders chosen, for obvious reasons as explored later.

Elders were chosen from among the people. They were known to Moses and were probably leaders in Egypt of various tribes or clans, under the domination of Pharaoh (not the best model, of course). It is very important that we understand that Moses chose the Elders of Israel.[2] They were not chosen by the people due to popularity, or through some electoral process. Because they were chosen by Moses, they were to become extensions of Moses' ministry, some of which did, some did not. They were under his authority. They were to act on his behalf in leading and caring for the people. Being chosen by Moses, they were to have Moses' concern first; they were to work for Moses and not the people.

As Moses chose these Elders, he did so with Jethro's recommendations in mind. The qualifications that Jethro gave Moses are well presented, but with a caution. Our process of choosing local elders is to be logical, as presented here, and Holy Spirit led.

> *"Such as fear God, men of truth, hating covetousness."*

The Elders were chosen "from the people." The heart of Eldership is to

---

[1] In *New Testament Pattern*, the church was seen in a geographical locality, e.g., Ephesus, Corinth, etc. This is the ideal, see *Supernatural Architecture*, DeKoven. Further, as will be presented later, New Testament elders were essentially pastors, bishops, etc. Thus, it is important not to take direct teaching from the Old Testament, but we must interpret the Old Testament in the light of New Testament revelation.

[2] However, the guidance of the Lord may have been absent in the process; again, see *Visionary Leadership*, DeKoven.

understand that as an Elder they are no longer "one of the people," but are an adjunct to the Fivefold Ministry gift leading the church; "a man under authority, having authority" (Matthew 8:9). (More on New Testament elders will follow).

Following this line of thought, "under authority, having authority" let's look at the second instance of the Old Testament pattern for New Testament Eldership (The more biblical pattern).

> In Numbers 11:16, the LORD therefore said to Moses, *"Gather for Me seventy men from the elders of Israel, whom you know to be the elders of the people and their officers and bring them to the tent of meeting, and let them take their stand there with you."* (NAS)

> This command of the Lord came after He presented His bitter complaint regarding the attitude of the people, lack of faith, and immature leadership.

> Numbers 11:24 – *"So Moses went out and told the people the words of the LORD. Also, he gathered seventy men of the elders of the people, and stationed them around the tent."* (NAS)

> Numbers 11:25 – *"Then the LORD came down in the cloud and spoke to him; and He took of the Spirit who was upon him and placed Him upon the seventy elders. And it came about that when the Spirit rested upon them, they prophesied. But they did not do it again."* (NAS)

> Numbers 11:30 – *"Then Moses returned to the camp, both he and the elders of Israel."* (NAS)

We see the pattern expanded from a different perspective; this time the Elders are known among the people and carry Moses' spirit or heart. Effective Elders are known not only by the ministry setting them in order, but also by the people whose lives they touch through faithful fulfillment of their Elder ministry.

The Elders were brought to the Tabernacle to stand with Moses. There God took the Spirit that was upon Moses and rested upon the sixty-eight who gathered there. The results were that their hearts were knit with the heart of Moses and they spoke the same vision and purpose. Elders are brought to the Tabernacle, the local church in geographic locality, to stand with the ministry and minister in the same spirit, saying the same thing. The pattern is confirmed by the two who remained in the camp, Eldad and Medad. Though they were not present at the Tabernacle they spoke with the same spirit as Moses and said the same thing. Even when we are not at the Tabernacle of the local church, Eldership must stand in unity and agreement in the direction of the ministry.

In the Old Testament, rulers (elders) were chosen from the people. They were men of maturity, functioning in a measure of leadership to give oversight and direction to God's people.

With some exceptions, to be noted in the next chapter, New Testament elders function in a similar manner. Though similar, there are significant and profound differences which can, will, and should affect the governance of the local church.

New Testament Elders

What Makes an Elder?

First, an elder meant one who was older, or mature. The New Testament model, at least initially, followed Hebrew tradition.

> 1 Timothy 3:1-7 – *"It is a trustworthy statement: if any man aspires to the office of overseer, it is a fine work he desires to do. 2 An overseer, then, must be above reproach, the husband of one wife, temperate, prudent, respectable, hospitable, able to teach, 3 not addicted to wine or pugnacious, but gentle, uncontentious, free from the love of money. 4 He must be one who manages his own household well, keeping his children under control with all dignity 5 (but if a man does not know how to manage his own household, how will he take care of the church of God?); 6 and not a new convert, lest he become conceited and fall into the condemnation incurred by the devil. 7 And he must have a good reputation with those outside the church, so that he may not fall into reproach and the snare of the devil."* (NAS)

The Bishop/Elder/Overseer/Pastor:

Terminology often changes and even the best of Bible scholars don't fully agree on the specific function of Bishops/Elders/Overseers/Pastors and Deacons as recorded in First Timothy. We do know that the Apostolic order of the first century church was much different than the government in most of our modern churches. Local churches were geographic rather than denominational or independent. The geographical churches were under the authority of the Apostolic ministries who founded them, who in turn worked together for the good of the church. Each geographical church had many local congregations over which a Bishop/Elder/Apostle/Pastor/Overseer presided. These Bishops/Elders, etc. were set in order by the Apostle who established the church (Acts 20:7, Titus 1:5, I Corinthians 4:18-21). For our purposes we will look at the qualities of both Bishop and Deacon and see how they apply today.

One caution should be noted. Jack Hayford made the point that these qualities are qualifications that we strive for. Since we are being progressively perfected we cannot view these qualities in a legalistic sense to qualify or disqualify on a single point. Rather we see these qualities as graces that we grow into as we mature in Christ and in the call to Eldership.

For convenience sake (mine) and to make this treatise a little more coherent, we will approach this passage as a word study.

What Is a Bishop/Elder?

Office of Bishop - episkope (ep-is-kop-ay'); inspection (for relief); by implication, superintendence; specially, the Christian "episcopate": KJV - office of a "bishop."

Eldership is an office that you are set into. The office confers a delegated authority and an anointing to fulfill the office. By definition Eldership is an "office of care" because the word Bishop means to inspect for relief, i.e., to see what needs to be done for someone or in the church. Elders may be set over specific areas of the church or over specific people or groups of people. Referring back to Titus 1:5 we see the Elders were set in order by the Apostolic ministry.

In most local congregations, there will likely be only one elder, usually the local church pastor. Pastors located in a locality would be the eldership of the church in the city. Other leaders in local congregations would be deacons or ministers.

Are You Qualified to Be a Bishop/Elder?

Desire-oregomai (or-eg'-o-mai); middle voice of apparently a prolonged form of an obsolete primary [compare 3735]; to stretch oneself, i.e., reach out after (long for): KJV - covet after, desire.

The central thought is "to stretch." I am certain that if you are an effective Elder you will be stretched by your office. Just as we grow in every other area of our Christian walk, we grow in areas of ministry. You are qualified to Eldership by the ministry that sets you into Eldership. Then by virtue of the authority and anointing delegated through the laying on of hands, (as well as prayer, experience, and study), you grow into your call as an Elder. No one is born mature, we all grow and in the process we often make mistakes. The successful Elder is one who learns from his or her mistakes, and in the process is stretched to maturity.

Have You Set Your Heart On Being An Elder?

Desireth - epithumeo (ep-ee-thoo-meh'-o); to set the heart upon, i.e., long for (rightfully or otherwise): KJV - covet, desire, would fain, lust (after).

I put a tremendous value on my ministry - to become President of the United States would be taking a step down from the calling of God on my life. How much value do you put on the ministry of an Elder? Effective Elders are always those who understand the value of ministry, both in the Kingdom of God and to themselves personally. Addressing the former, we need good Elders in the church; men and women who love God, love people, and love the work of the ministry. An effective Eldership multiplies the effectiveness of the leadership in the church of the locality. In looking at the latter, there are several personal reasons that one can attach to the ministry of Eldership; personal satisfaction in helping people's lives, having a more active role in building the Kingdom of God, the standing that Eldership confers on you among the people, and not least of all the promise of eternal reward. To put it simply, God blesses those who are faithful in the Eldership! If you don't value Eldership, you are not an Elder.

What Does an Elder Do?

A Bishop - episkopos (ep-is'-kop-os); a superintendent, i.e., Christian officer in genitive case charge of a (or the) church (literally or figuratively): KJV - bishop, overseer. In our modern church life, the title of Bishop is one of prestige, power and position. Sadly, rather than seeing Bishop as a function with responsibility, it is presented as a title with rights and privileges. How far we have regressed from New Testament understandings.

The Eldership, by definition, is a working position and not just a title. Too often, immature people want the title without wanting the responsibility; the two go hand in hand. As an Elder you will be called on to function in overseeing areas of ministry, serve communion, and preach the Word, etc. There is a time demand and a price to be paid for the office.

In theory, Eldership also serves as an advisory board to an Apostolic team. Often times, as God leads an Apostle, he seeks the wisdom of the Eldership for their unique perspectives. We always seek a consensus among our Eldership as we move forward for God. In the event that a consensus cannot be reached among the Eldership, we set ourselves in agreement with the Apostle. In all things we always seek the good of the kingdom of God and His purpose.

What Character Traits Should Be Developed As an Elder?

The characteristics of an Elder/Deacon are discussed most fully in Paul's letter to Timothy, and are discussed here (I Tim. 3:1-13).

1. An Elder Is Blameless.
Blameless – [anepileptos (an-ep-eel'-ape-tos)]; not arrested, i.e., (by implication) inculpable: KJV - blameless, unrebukable.

There are always those who will find fault in a leader. For that reason it is very important that Elders live lives in accordance with the Word of God. We must pay our bills, manage our affairs, and be the sole of discretion, so that faultfinders and accusers have no real basis for their fault finding and accusations.

16

2. An Elder Is Sober Minded.

Sober - sophron - safe (sound) in mind, i.e., self-controlled (moderate as to opinion or passion): KJV - discreet, sober, temperate.

There are a multitude of applications for the word sober. We think of someone who is dour in appearance and seldom laughs, yet Jesus began His ministry by attending a wedding feast and turning the water into wine. Our definition of sober then must be temperance in personality and pursuits. Our opinions are important, but not important to the point of strife. Our passions must be moderated by the call to the office. Eldership is not for the flighty or fickle, neither is it for the rigid or repressed; Eldership is for those who have found a balance in life, a balance between passion and maturity.

3. An Elder Is on His or Her "Best Behavior."

Of Good Behavior – [kosmios (kos'-mee-os)]; orderly, i.e., decorous: KJV - of good behavior, modest.

Another way of saying "good behavior" is "well mannered." A mature Elder knows how to conduct his or herself in public without embarrassing either the Kingdom of God or the Five-Fold leadership. A wise Elder knows when to speak and when to hold their peace with decorum.

4. An Elder Must Love People!

Given to Hospitality - philoxenos; fond of guests, i.e. hospitable: KJV - given to (lover of, uses) hospitality.

Elders must be people persons, because people are what the church is all about. One pastor said, "I love the ministry, it's the people that I can't stand!" But the ministry is all about people in all shapes, sizes, and temperaments. Good people, bad people, the righteous, and the religious. The hospitable Elder meets people where they are, always recognizing that people are people and they will always be people.

5. An Elder Must Be Able to Teach.

Apt to Teach – [didaktikos (did-ak-tik-os')]; instructive ("didactic"): KJV - apt to teach.

By word and deed, exhortation and example, an Elder is a teacher. An elder should be able to teach from behind a lectern or pulpit, and to teach in counsel and communication, in attitudes and actions. An Elder must be "apt to teach." Our teaching should always be with purpose, to fulfill the goals of God (I Tim. 1:5).

6. An Elder Should Not Be A Drunkard.
Not Given to Wine [paroinos (par'-oy-nos)]; staying near wine, KJV - given to wine.

We will look at this from two perspectives. Drinking (or not drinking) alcoholic beverages is more a matter of custom and conviction than biblical command. Jesus told the Pharisees, "The Son of Man comes both eating and drinking and you say behold a man gluttonous and a winebibber." The Bible makes it clear that we are to be moderate in every aspect of our lives. A drunkard cannot effectively serve as an Elder and a leader among the people.

Having established the principle, let's carry it a step farther - there are more ways to be drunk than on wine. There are those who are drunk on the cares of this world, with climbing the corporate ladder, and keeping up with the Joneses. Remember that the scriptures tell us –

> *"But seek ye first the kingdom of God and His righteousness and all of these other things shall be added unto thee."* (Matthew 6:33, KJV)

An effective Elder lives and enjoys a balanced abundant life.

7. An Elder Should Not Be Quarrelsome.
No Striker – [plektes (plake'-tace)]; from 4141; pugnacious (quarrelsome): KJV - striker.

As ludicrous as it may seem, more than one church board meeting has ended in a fistfight. When unqualified people exercise positions of leadership, anything can happen.

An effective Elder must not be quarrelsome. There may be times that one has to be forthright and stand firm on conviction, right or wrong, but there is a vast difference between standing firm and starting (or fueling) an argument. A wise man or woman never argues - to argue is to have already lost the battle.

8. An Elder Has Proper Motivation.
Not Greedy of Filthy Lucre [aphilarguros (af-il-ar'-goo-ros)]; unavaricious: KJV - without covetousness, not greedy of filthy lucre.

The attitude of greed is the thing that causes the lucre (money) to become filthy. Money in and of itself is neither good nor evil; it is the attitude toward money that determines good or evil. Interestingly enough, lack of money rather then abundance is what usually leads to avariciousness and greed. When one has a proper concept of money it becomes a tool to meet the need - whether of the kingdom, the needs of others, or personal needs.

An effective Elder guards against greed. At the same time, an effective Elder knows his or her heart. There are many motivations that motivate us. Some are primary motivations, some are secondary. Our primary motivations must be: loving God, faithful obedience, and loving people. Our secondary motivations may be as varied as our personalities: affirmation, love of action, sense of accomplishment, and others that may pertain just to you. As we honestly search our hearts to know our own motivations we become more effective for God and less inclined to fall into the condemnation of the devil.

9. An Elder Is Patient.
Patient – [epieikes (ep-ee-i-kace')]; appropriate, i.e., (by implication) mild: KJV - gentle; moderation, patient, sweet reasonableness[3]

Many of us have prayed in our frustration, "Lord give me patience and give it to me now!" Adversity came and with it we learned patience. Never pray for patience; this is one grace that you need to develop on your own.

As an Elder you need to develop patience. You will need patience in dealing with God's people, who are often difficult, at best, to deal with.

---

[3] See Dr. Ken Chant's seminal work on this topic, presented brilliantly in his book *Christian Life: Patterns of Gracious Living.*

Often it takes patience to build a struggling ministry in the church. Patience will cause you to possess promises after others have given up trying. Patience will cause you to possess your soul and lead you to an eternal reward. Be patient; God has been patient with us...His mercies are new every morning!

10. An Elder Is Peaceable.
Not a Brawler [amachos (am'-akh-os)]; peaceable: KJV - not a brawler.

In looking at this word in the Greek it is interesting to see how close it is in pronunciation to the word, "macho." We don't need macho Elders who feel that they have to prove themselves. This attitude reflects a lack of inner peace, and an insecurity which leads to conflict.

A phrase that I keep finding myself repeating is, "So what's the big deal?" This is usually in conjunction with some molehill that someone has magnified into a mountain. Many people live lives of constant frustration because they have no inner peace; they lack a basic trust in God's goodness and grace. An effective Elder first has peace with God (Romans 5:1) and then peace with others. The attitude of peace will carry you through the aggravations of life and enable you to execute your Eldership from a position of strength. Remember - a perspective of peace enables you to solve the problem, not become a part of it.

11. An Elder Is Not Covetous.
Not Covetous – [aphilarguros (af-il-ar'-goo-ros)]; unavaricious: KJV - without covetousness, not greedy of filthy lucre.

Since this is the same word used in number eight, we must look to the translators for insight. Covetousness goes far beyond your neighbor's wealth or wife (or husband). A person can be covetous of position and power. There have been Elders who have coveted the Senior Leader's position, or the relationship that exists within the staff. Leaders must not covet what someone else has, whether it is money, a wife, position, or power. An effective Elder realizes that there will always be people with more and there will always be people with less. Whether more or less we need to be comfortable with our place in God and our place in the church, always striving to be the best that we can be and have the best that we can have while rejoicing at what God does in and for the lives of others. As the great theologian Clint Eastwood once said, "A man's got to know his limitations." Of course, Mr. Eastwood is an actor/director, not a theologian, but the statement is true. We all have limitations. A key to success in leadership is to know our gifts and calling and function according to the measure of grace God has given.

12. An Elder Has Order at Home.
Rule Over [proistemi (pro-is'-tay-mee)]; to stand before, i.e. (in rank) to preside, or (by implication) to practice: KJV - maintain, be over, rule.

This is a practical requirement. If your home is in constant turmoil, you cannot be an effective Elder. This doesn't mean that there won't or can't be problems in your home - it does mean that you must do something about the problems, dealing with them in an effective, scriptural way.

13. An Elder Cannot Be a Novice.
Not a Novice – [neophutos (neh-of'-oo-tos)]; newly, planted, i.e., (figuratively) a young convert ("neophyte"): KJV - novice.

There are a number of reasons that immediately come to mind for the prohibition of novices being Elders. Lack of biblical knowledge, stability, strength, and a host of others. There is, however, one overriding reason - maturity; in Christ and in life. An Elder must be filled with a certain amount of wisdom that comes only with age. An Elder by definition is an "Elder" and not a novice. Your Eldership is proved by your maturity in dealing with people and problems. Elders are called upon by Senior Ministry to give their wisdom in matters relating to the church; whereas, a novice might see the immediacy of the question, a mature Elder, in wisdom, grasps the big picture and gives cogent counsel from his or her perspective.

14. An Elder Must Have a Good Report.
Good Report – [marturia (mar-too-ree-ah)]; evidence given (judicially or genitive case): KJV - record, report, testimony, witness.

Specifically, a good report from those who are without, i.e., outside the church. Elders must have a reputation for honoring their word, paying their bills, and conducting the business of life in an honorable way. When choosing Elders, it is recommended for Five-Fold ministers to check a prospective Elder's reputation at work, in the world. Many problems could be avoided if we chose Elders that do not just look good at church, but are good in reputation in the world. Eldership doesn't demand perfection. But it does demand personal integrity. The man or woman of integrity will have a good report from, and the respect of, the community in which they live.

The reason that an Elder must have a good report of those without is because we don't want to fall into condemnation as a church, even as we don't want our Elders to be condemned over their public behavior or reputation.

It is our purpose to always work toward restoration of anyone who falls into sin, while remembering the words of the Paul the Apostle,

> *"Do not receive an accusation against an elder except on the basis of two or three witnesses."* (1 Timothy 5:19, NAS)

The nature of your place in ministry means that there is always potential to either cause offense, or through misunderstanding to cause reproach. We will not and cannot listen to every idle word spoken against an Elder. If you hear an accusation against an Elder you need to deal with it immediately by taking the accuser to the accused privately. Deal with it and go on in God.

It is important that those in Eldership do all they can within the limits of human frailty to avoid bringing shame or embarrassment to the church.

A Recent Story

Just recently two incidents requiring intervention occurred near our city. The first involved a local elder (Pastor) who had been accused by a rumor of misappropriating church funds. When the accusation was made, rather than passing on or ignoring the rumor, two acting elders brought the accuser to the accused elder to confront the matter. Evidence was produced to clear the name of the elder, and the problem was solved.

A second incident did not turn out as well. A local elder was accused of immoral behavior. This time, it was not one but three accusers, and our local eldership determined upon a thorough investigation that sadly it was true. The elder was asked to step down from leadership, which began a long, arduous but ultimately fruitful restoration process for the elder, his family, and the local congregation.

"There are two kinds of leaders: those who are interested in the flock, and those who are interested in the fleece."

- Anonymous

CHAPTER 2

PRACTICAL APPLICATION OF ELDER PRINCIPLES

Primary Responsibility

The primary responsibility of an Elder is to the Senior Minister or Senior Pastor of the church (unless you are the minister). As Aaron and Hur held up Moses' hands in the battle against the Amalekites, and Israel prevailed, so must local church leaders hold up the hands of an Apostolic Leader. Your job is not to serve "the institutional church" nor is it your job to serve the people. Saul served the people and lost a kingdom. Absolom started serving the people and ignited a rebellion. You will be involved in ministry to the people, but the primary responsibility is to the Apostle/Senior Leader/Five-Fold Ministry/other Elder in the locality.

Maturity

The essence of Eldership is maturity, both spiritual and emotional. It takes both to understand and accept the role of an Elder. Spiritually and emotionally mature people are able to assume responsibilities, work to solve problems, and work with others for the glory of God.

A spiritually immature person who attempts to fulfill an Elder's position often has difficulty submitting his or herself to spiritual authority. As a result, they may cause confusion in the church. It has been my experience that emotionally immature people have conflict with others, both inside and outside of the Eldership, because of their own insecurities. There is no place for the spiritually or emotionally immature in Eldership.

There is a sense of stature and stability that a secure, mature person has. That sense of security and maturity inspires others to follow their leadership and example. The mature leader finds a need and fills it - understanding the vision, while working to see it fulfilled.

Keeping a Sense of Vision

Eldership is responsible to present and to promote the vision to the congregation. The vision is summed up differently by different congregations. Here is a sample:

1. To Establish a Pattern Church Incorporating Apostolic Anointing and Authority
2. To Build Strong Believers, Mature in Faith and Action
3. To Touch People at Their Need
4. To Reach the City for God, through Effective Life and Witness
5. To Build a Platform for National Ministry
6. To Be on the Cutting Edge of All That God Is Doing and Saying

There may be those who rise up in the congregation to challenge the vision and cause division. Promote the vision! By promoting the vision you are promoting unity in the congregation, creating anticipation for greater things in God, and channeling believers into productive areas of service. One Church/One Vision! One Purpose, led by the Holy Spirit!

Giving Wise Counsel

> Proverbs 15:22… *"Without consultation, plans are frustrated, but with many counselors they succeed."*

Eldership serves as an advisory counsel to the Apostolic Leadership in a locality. Wise counsel is always needed and frequently different people have different perspectives that can bring valuable insight as problems are examined and policies set. A ministry team should always seek unanimity, but if a consensus is not reached the Eldership will need Apostolic insight to keep things in order, often provided through an Advisory Presbytery or an Apostolic council.

When We Need New Elders

The process for finding Elders for the church is simple - find someone who is already doing the job and then give them the position.

The Apostle is responsible for opening the Eldership to new Elders. The Elders may nominate candidates, who will be discussed by the Eldership.

If everyone seems to be of one mind, the prospective Elder(s) will be contacted and given information on their roles and responsibilities.[4] Prospective Elders will be asked if they can fulfill their responsibilities and if they desire the office. If the answer is affirmative, the Apostle and Eldership will set the Elder(s) in place during a special service and they will take their place among the Elder(s). (Usually as a "staff pastor" or in a new church plant).

An Elder Has Responsibilities

An Elder is to work. If one has the title, they must do the job. Responsibilities are many. Elders are a part of the leadership team and as such function as a Pastor/Shepherd does. The responsibilities can include:

- Elders are responsible for follow-up of visitors and absentees.
- Elders may be called upon to give counsel to members.
- Elders may be called upon to pray for the sick at the end of a service or in the hospital.
- Elders are responsible for meeting in prayer for the Sunday services.
- Elders represent the Apostle or Senior Pastor to the congregation.
- Elders are responsible for confronting problems in love and dealing with the discontented.
- Elders keep the vision before the people.
- Elders may be placed over various ministries in the church as overseers.
- Elders are to be above reproach (1 Timothy 3:2; Titus 1:6; 1 Timothy 3:9).
- Elders must be husbands of one wife (not polygamous) (1 Timothy 3:2; Titus 1:6; 1 Timothy 3:12).
- Elders must be temperate (1 Timothy 3:2; Titus 1:7; 1 Timothy 3:8)
- Elders must be respectable (1 Timothy 3:2; 1 Timothy 3:8)
- Elders must not be given to drunkenness (1 Timothy 3:3; Titus 1:7; 1 Timothy 3:8).
- Elders must be able to manage their own families well (1 Timothy 3:4; 1 Timothy 3:12).
- Elders must see that their children are obedient (1 Timothy 3:4-5; Titus 1:6; 1 Timothy 3:12).
- Elders must not pursue dishonest gain (Titus 1:7; 1 Timothy 3:8).
- Elders hold to the truth (Titus 1:9; 1 Timothy 3:8).

---

[4] Such as found in this book.

- Elders are not overbearing (Titus 1:7).
- Elders are not quick-tempered (Titus 1:7).
- Elders are lovers of what is good (Titus 1:8).
- Elders are upright and holy (Titus 1:8).
- Elders are disciplined (Titus 1:8).

* The most important responsibility that an Elder has is to hold up the Apostle's or Senior Pastor's hands in ministry.

If an Elder takes these responsibilities to heart, the church will grow and prosper and the needs of the people will be met.

Are There Any Other Special Requirements?

Absolutely! An Elder is expected to give leadership help in most church services and activities.[5] Although one must recognize that jobs, vacations, and special activities may cause an Elder to miss services, the expectation is that Elders are to be in all main services as leaders. In the event that an Elder is not able to attend services or is leaving town; it would be helpful if they contact other leaders to insure the ministry's flow and function.

Further, Elders are scheduled to give communion to the congregation. This is a most sacred rite of the church. Communion time is a special focus of the worship experience. Elders are expected to be instant in season and out of season and may be called upon to perform many of the responsibilities of ministry.

The Elders Walk With God

This brings us to the most important part of an Elder's life and ministry - their personal walk with God. An Elder who is slack in his or her spiritual life becomes ineffectual as an Elder and is often used by the enemy to cause confusion and contention in the Eldership and in the church. Moses' first qualification, as advised by Jethro (good advice), was that Elders fear God; in our day the first qualification should be that an Elder love God by keeping Jesus' commandments (i.e., to fear God). If a leader of any dimension has a true love for God they will maintain communion and fellowship with God. Elders are encouraged to be men and women of

---

[5] See *Pastoral Leadership* by Dr. Stan DeKoven

prayer, attentive to the Word, worshippers of God who have learned the secret of waiting on the Lord. Thus, it is important to remember the words of Isaiah 40:31:

> *"But they that wait upon the Lord shall renew their strength, they shall mount up on wings as eagles, they shall run and not be weary, they shall walk and not faint."*

Lord teach us to wait!

Stepping Up or Stepping Down

Over the life of the church in locality, there will be a number of Elders promoted in the ministry. Eldership is often a training time for the Five - Fold ministry. If full-time ministry is the goal and desire of a man or woman of God, the Lord saying the same thing, faithfulness in the Eldership will prove one's ministry before God and man. Faithfulness brings promotion.

There are times when due to sickness, personal problems, and other circumstances, an Elder wishes to step down from the position. It must be understood that circumstances change and if an Elder wishes to step down for an indefinite period of time, their wish should be honored. If circumstances change and the Eldership is again desired, the individual should be reconsecrated to the position of Elder.

A Final Word

All of this sounds like a lot of work with a little reward. On the contrary: Eldership is a lot of work with a lot of reward. First, there is the reward of service well done. The day will come when every faithful servant of God will hear the words that they have labored to hear:

> *"Well done thou good and faithful servant, enter thou into the joy of thy Lord."* - Matthew 25:21, KJV

Heaven will be a wonderful place of eternal reward. What one sows on earth will be reaped in eternity. Secondly, God blesses the faithful on earth. Most Elders can vocationally report the blessing of God in their lives, testifying with the Psalmist:

"I have seen the goodness of the Lord in the land of the living." (Psalm 27:13)

Further, there is the joy of being a part of a ministry that is doing the work of fulfilling the purposes of God (Hab. 2:14). Most will agree that the rewards of Eldership are worth the price of admission.

"Christianity has always been a community – operated faith."

- Henry Klapp

CHAPTER 3

DEACONS: THE BUSINESS OF CHURCH LIFE

Now with these truths in mind, it is necessary to turn to the qualifications for Deacons, or business leaders as Paul called them. To do so, one must also bear in mind that in today's complex society there may be certain other practical and proficiency requirements as well to insure that the business and legal matters of the church are handled well. Paul simply stated what was needed for their appointment, in terms of spiritual and social requirements, as he did for Elders.

Honor

The office of such persons is not to be taken lightly - it is an office of honor and responsibility. (Consider the Apostolic directive in I Tim. 3:13.)

Responsibilities

Repeatedly, Deacons or Deaconesses have asked the question, "Now that I am appointed what am I supposed to do?" That, of course, is a sign of willingness to follow with a willing heart. The person who will not take counsel is dangerous. This section is presented to introduce the responsibilities of a Business Deacon.

What They Are and What They Are Not

The Deacon's responsibilities are indicated in Acts 6, and are spelled out in most local Churches' Bylaws. Consider the sample found in the back of this book. Under no conditions, scripturally nor legally, are Deacons to assume they are the Pastor's "boss." Nothing in church life is more frightening than to have a "deacon possessed church"; a demon-possessed church can be dealt with...cast the demons out! But deacons...sometimes they are the greatest devil's advocate in church life. Scripturally, and according to most well written Church Bylaws (legally), the Pastor/Five-Fold Ministry is of necessity the head of the church under Christ. Of course, that does not mean that he/she can become a dictator, nor that his/her conduct cannot be questioned when danger signs appear. Well written Bylaws will clearly spell out the procedures for properly handling Senior Ministry misconduct.

Jesus left His Church the Great Commission and every officer of the New Testament Church is assigned the responsibility of facilitating that Commission. Any other purpose of serving is unworthy of consideration. As the Church develops, they must adopt procedures to cause the Church to operate smoothly and effectively. This is administration, and administration is a necessary component for church life. (See Romans 12:8, Lead or Administrate)

Relationships

Ministry is all about relationships. Let us consider the importance of relationships as seen in:

1. To one another

There is to be a brotherhood, a common interest and mutual respect in life and ministry. There is no place for ego, or the manifestation of selfish interests in church life. Each Deacon is a member of the team and they must conduct themselves accordingly. Since all are servants of God and the body of believers, relationships should be filled with kindness and sweet reasonableness.

2. To the membership

Deacons represent the membership, but not exclusively. So does the leadership and other officers of the church. The Deacon is accountable to the membership morally, ethically, and legally for its action. Generally, the Deacons are not a legislative body, although they may have limited legislative powers within the scope of their authority. It is, as a rule, an administrative body, designed to facilitate the work of God in a locality.

3. To the Spiritual/Five Fold Ministry Leaders

Originally, such officers were appointed by the minister. That would, of course, make them accountable to their appointee. Many church Bylaws specifically state the Deacon is to assist the Pastor/Apostle in the administrative duties of the church. They do not, however, have the responsibility to intervene when irregularities begin to crop up here and there. They should act according to Scripture and in keeping with the church's legal documents.[6]

Qualifications

The characteristics for a Deacon/Deaconess are similar to an Elder, but with some distinct differences. One distinctive is that Elders must be able to teach, where as, Deacons may or may not be similarly gifted.

Specifically, Deacons must:

- Be above reproach (blameless) (1 Timothy 3:2; Titus 1:6; 1 Timothy 3:9).
- Be a spouse of one husband/wife (1 Timothy 3:2; Titus 1:6; 1 Timothy 3:12).
- Be temperate (1 Timothy 3:2; Titus 1:7; 1 Timothy 3:8).
- Be respectable (1 Timothy 3:2; 1 Timothy 3:8).
- Be not given to drunkenness (1 Timothy 3:3; Titus 1:7; 1 Timothy 3:8).
- Be able to manage his own family well (1 Timothy 3:4; 1 Timothy 3:12).
- Seeing that his children are obedient (1 Timothy 3:4-5; Titus 1:6; 1 Timothy 3:12).
- Does not pursue dishonest gain (Titus 1:7; 1 Timothy 3:8).
- Holds to the truth (Titus 1:9; 1 Timothy 3:9).
- Be sincere (1 Timothy 3:8).
- Be tested (1 Timothy 3:10).

As with Elders, Deacons serve under Senior leadership to facilitate the work of ministry. However, differently than Elders/Overseers/Pastors, Deacons care for the business functions, from finances to maintenance to various support activities. The position of Deacon is an awesome responsibility of God, is not for the faint-hearted, but for the mature believer gifted in serving.

---

[6] More on Controlling Documents in the chapter to follow, Strategic Planning.

"You don't have to plan to fail; all you have to do is fail to plan."

- Anonymous

CHAPTER 4

ADMINISTRATIVE OPERATIONS: STRATEGIC PLANNING AND THE CHURCH

It has been appropriately stated that if one fails to plan, they plan to fail. In my years of Kingdom service, the greatest problem in terms of burnout in ministry and a general lack of growth in the work of God comes because of a lack of positive, purposeful planning.

Assuming a solid apostolic (governmentally and doctrinally sound) and prophetic (vision) foundation has been laid to a ministry, administration must follow to prepare for greater growth. When I state administration, I do not mean institutionalization or denominationalism, for the very purpose of these entities is by definition the perpetuation of themselves. They tend to be difficult to change when change is needed (not change merely for the sake of change). What I do mean is the organization of the living organism (lively stones) called the Church, body of Christ, family of God, Army of the Lord. All four of these metaphors used in scripture to describe Christian life together requires executive function (head) and basic organization. Thus, whether your overall structure is program or cell oriented, structure or organization are needed in preparation for growth. It all starts with a vision and mission mandate.

Prayer & Questions

When called upon to bring structure to any organization, especially a local congregation, much prayer is needed, and certain questions must be asked and answered. Prayer is for wisdom, questions asked are related to the reason (other than corporate) for the existence of the work. All ministries, to be a viable force for God, must have a vision and mission statement that is clear and understandable, which is written and proclaimed. A sample of a mission/vision statement can be found in Illustration 1 (page 45).

Following the mission statement should be broad, achievable objectives that flow from the vision/mission and values of the ministry. Such statements as "win the world for Christ" are great but not that helpful.

Objectives are broad statements focused on a vision of God for your ministry.

Then come goals, which are overall, and departmental. Even in cell churches, there are still departments (such as the "music cell" or "youth cell") where leadership is needed and goals are to be established. The goals to be set will always relate to the greater goals, which in turn relate to the mission and vision, and are explicitly presented in the position descriptions for the ministry department. (See Illustration 2, page 46)

I mention position or ministry position here for emphasis. One complaint registered by non-clergy leadership in local congregations is that, though they want to serve and do so effectively in church life, they commonly do not know what the expectations and purposes are for their serving. Though the church is not a business, it by necessity needs to run on sound business principles. One would not start a new job without knowing the requirements of the job (caution, flexibility is always helpful especially as a volunteer worker). Thus, the need for a ministry/position description that outlines such duties and focuses on achieving a worthwhile, godly aim is key.

Of course, when establishing goals, whether corporate or departmental, prayer and input from the workers is important. Hopefully, once the "big picture" vision and mission, along with overall goals are established by senior leaders, the workers will be challenged (with a time frame for completion) to put in writing their specific goals for their area of responsibility. These goals should be evaluated and mutually agreed upon by the worker and supervisor. Goals should be faith-filled and realistic and must, at all times, be measurable. In other words, measurable and realistic goals provide the framework for relational accountability in the ministry, which is vital to establish and maintain a healthy department/work.

Goals are great, but without implementation they become nice charts with limited meaning. A plan for implementation must be established which is related to the goal (or task) and is to be approached as a problem to be solved. For example, if a young woman had been called upon to teach a Sunday School class of 8 year old boys and girls, she would (hopefully) have a written position description with goals, and purposes that relate to the overall mission of the church (Matt. 28:16-20). She would then, challenged by her supervisor, be tasked with solving the problem of achieving the goal of increasing the 8 year old class by 20% (in this case, from 10 to 12 students). The process for determining the plan of implementation is best done using a sample problem solving technique called "brainstorming." In brainstorming the task (20% growth) is presented as a problem, and <u>any</u> possible solution is explored. The options presented can range from the ridiculous (kidnap 2 kids from XYZ Church down the road) to the sublime (helping the other 8-year-olds invite friends to a special backyard party to share the gospel with them). No possible solution is dismissed out of hand (well, perhaps the kidnapping one) and the most logical one(s) are then chosen to implement. Along with the problem solving process, logistical planning (time, budget, transportation, obstacles to achieving goal, etc.) are discussed and presented. Through this process, plans that focus toward achieving goals which will fulfill a part of the mission/vision of the ministry are established. But, of course, you then have to work the plan.

Working the Plan

Working the plan is not always easy. Often in life and ministry opposition arises. This should not surprise us, as every ministry ordained of God will go through times of testing, for numerous reasons (test our faithfulness, etc.). However, assuming your goals and plan are realistic and implementable (your supervisor should be able to help with that) working the plan means to work through the problems that present themselves. One of the greatest obstacles for workers today is the lack of perceived or real support (budget, emotional, affirmation, etc.) for the work given. Entrepreneurialship is almost absent today, due to several reasons. In the past, generations (especially our World War II era patriots) had a sense that if a job was worth doing it was worth doing well, and, if the resources were not readily available to complete a task, they would find the resources. That attitude is unfortunately lacking for most volunteers. However, lack is the reality for most ministries, and thus, between the supervisor and worker, resources must be found to implement the plan to achieve success (seeing two precious 8 year olds come to Christ and begin a life-long love relationship with Christ and his Body).

Core Values

Another important item to have in the planning process is core values. Successful people in all walks of life have mastered the task of determining their core values (what they really believe and want) match their life pattern (their work, priorities, time, etc). One reason goals are not well achieved may be that there is a conflict between a core value (e.g., I want to be a Sunday School teacher because it is important) and (I want to develop my social life by being with friends until 2 AM Sunday morning). Our core values, derived (hopefully) from scriptural principles, and our work/ministry activity (where we actually commit our resources) need to be congruent wherever possible.

Finally, as a part of a strategic plan, feedback, or evaluation for correction and improvement is to be an ongoing process. Any document from an organizational chart (see Illustration 3, page 48) to position descriptions and vision strategies are living documents, historical and faith focused. As a living document, it presents the core values, mission and vision, along with general guidelines and goals. But, as time marches on, and the needs of the ministry life change, so must our overall strategic plan and all individual plans contained as a part of the overriding strategic plan. This is best done through times of refreshing, staff or department meetings, retreats (or advances if you must) or informal times where the goals and plans are reviewed and modified as needed. Feedback, knowing how we are doing, accolades for the achieved and encouragement or reassignment for the non-achievers is considered. All of God's people should desire to grow and improve for Christ's sake. Feedback, both encouraging and disheartening, help to determine our effectiveness and determine our willingness to work in a specific area of service. Personally, I have started more than one endeavor with enthusiasm and faith, only to realize a few months down the road that the job and I were ill suited for each other. This is not a tragedy, only a glitch that with loving supervision can be corrected for the benefit of all.

Once all the data is gathered from workers, departments, etc., it is then to be placed in a notebook for the Elders/Deacons to use as a living document for the management of the ministry. These notebooks or portfolios provide everyone the opportunity to "sing off the same sheet of music" as far as church life goes, and all workers should have a modified and simplified version of the whole document, that specifically speaks to the department or ministry in which they serve. Of course, the work of organization is not yet done. As a part of the implementing for ministry, there comes a need for policy and procedural guidelines to be developed. In the beginning of a ministry, policies and procedures can be kept to a minimum (as required by law and prudence). But as a work grows to ease communication, enhance efficiency and minimize conflicts, various policies and procedures for operation can and should be implemented. The potential reach of these policies and procedures are beyond the scope of this book, but a few samples are provided later. For comprehensive policies and procedures it is recommended that the reader obtain the CD by Dr. Howard Ryan, Church Enrichment Ministries, available through Vision Publishing.[7]

A strategic plan takes work, lots of work. But it is worth it. Remember, a strategic plan is a living document, to be used as a guide under the rule of God's Word and Spirit. All ministries need one to more effectively implement Kingdom business.

Illustration 1

Vision: Take the Whole Word to the Whole World...Equipping God's Leaders

Mission: To establish educational ministries in cooperative local churches world wide, and provide resources to fulfill the vision.

Objective/Purpose:

1. Write, print, and distribute books, study guides to equip leaders world wide.

2. Prepare men and women for leadership in the world through various teaching modalities.

Goals:

1. To increase our campus network by 20 percent.

---

[7] See end of this book for ordering information.

2. To increase student body by 10 percent.

3. To write and print five new books.

4. To translate five new books into Spanish, Russian, French, etc.

Plan for Implementation:

1. Increase networking marketing.

2. Prioritize writing projects; take two months sabbatical to complete projects.

Core Values:

1. Minister grace with emphasis on restoration and equipping.

2. Minister integrity in all business dealings.

Feedbacks:

1. Quarterly meeting of all staff.

2. Bi-monthly staff meeting.

3. Annual meeting with Executive Coach/Strategic Planner – Institute for Leadership Training.

Illustration 2

Ministry Position Description

Position: Home Fellowship Pastor

Supervisor: Associate Pastor

Responsibilities: To lead a home fellowship on behalf of the church with duties to include facilitation, teaching, praying, or counseling.

Goals:

1. To increase members by 20%.
2. To train an assistant with the goal of starting new Home Fellowships.
3. Receive 10 hours of training via Vision International University.

Plan for Achieving Goals:

1. Begin Fellowship January 5.
2. Start meeting with potential new leader by March 10.
3. Enroll in Vision by January 5.

Review Process/Re-evaluation:

1. Monthly/quarterly meeting with supervisor for evaluation
2. Weekly report to be submitted to supervisor

Illustration 3

This is our Vision Organizational Chart

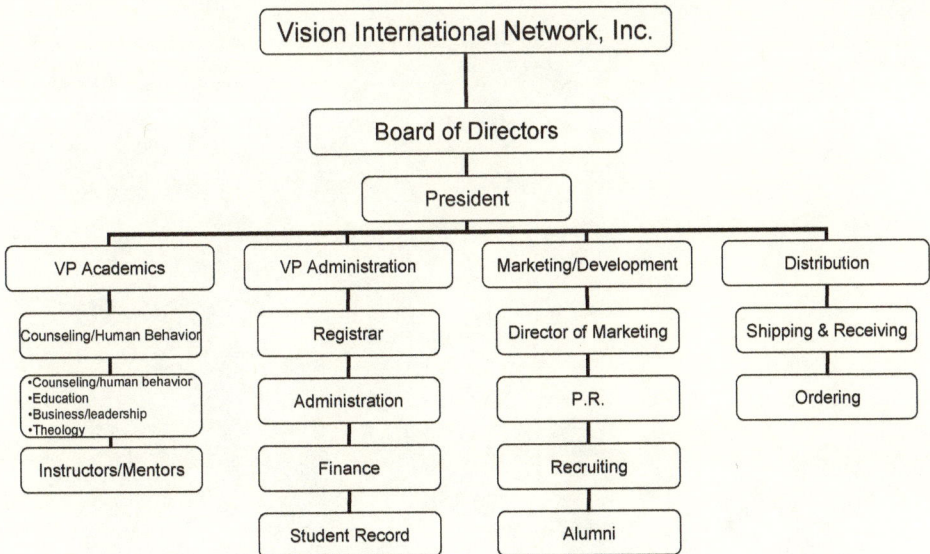

```
                    Vision International Network, Inc.
                                  |
                          Board of Directors
                                  |
                             President
        _____|_____
        |               |                    |               |
   VP Academics    VP Administration   Marketing/Development  Distribution
        |               |                    |               |
Counseling/Human    Registrar         Director of Marketing  Shipping & Receiving
  Behavior             |                    |                  |
  •Counseling/human  Administration        P.R.              Ordering
   behavior             |                    |
  •Education          Finance            Recruiting
  •Business/leadership   |                    |
  •Theology          Student Record       Alumni
        |
Instructors/Mentors
```

"The work is never finished until the paperwork is done."

- Anonymous

CHAPTER 5

CONTROLLING DOCUMENTS OF THE CHURCH

There are basically five documents of legal consequence in church control. They are all created by the local congregation and for the local congregation, and they are not only invaluable in promoting orderly procedure, they are of utmost importance in legal matters as well. They must be considered from at least three positions: 1) The Bible pattern and purpose; 2) Practicality; 3) Legal requirements.

The Constitution

The Constitution contains the founding principles of a not-for-profit organization. These should be kept to a minimum in content, leaving the details of operational procedure to other areas such as the Bylaws and minutes. Matters of faith should be left to still another document - "The Articles of Faith."

The Constitution should contain the basic foundation of an organization as follows:

I. Name
II. Purpose
III. Place of Business (optional)
IV. Membership
V. Officers
VI. Meetings (business)
VII. Amendment Method
VIII. Dissolution Clause (optional)

The Dissolution Clause must be in the Articles of Incorporation for Internal Revenue Service approval (for U.S. corporations). It is not essential to place it in the Constitution, but it is a good practice. Of course, in many nations, an official trust, corporation, etc., is not required; some other legal instrument is needed. However, even where an official document is not required, an unofficial document modeled after this is helpful for planning purposes.

51

Bylaws

The Bylaws contain operational procedures and must be more detailed than the Constitution. They are designed for the implementation of the organization's purpose and must be in harmony with the Constitution and the Articles of Incorporation from which they derive their authority. Included in them should be ways and means of doing business, including elections (if any), terms for officers, membership meetings, etc. (a sample of Bylaws is found on page 61). A third instrument of importance is the Agenda for meetings to conduct church business. These are important as they provide guidelines for discussion, keeping an order for fluid dialog and decision. A typical Agenda may include:

A G E N D A - Board of Elders Meeting, January 16, 2002

(Example)

I. Call to order (That is, to start meeting).

II. Prayer and Devotions (Led by someone on the Board).

III. Roll Call (of all present & absent).

IV. Agenda (which should be in writing prior to the meeting, and kept on file with the minutes).

V. Minutes (read from the previous meeting, to insure accuracy).

VI. Financial Report (How much, what is spent & where).

VII. Unfinished Business

    1. Proposed heating system, repair for sanctuary

    2. Increase of Deacons for church growth

    3. Special meetings with Evangelist John Doe

VIII. New Business

    1. The need for Nursery help

    2. Vehicle replacement for Youth Ministry

    3. Establish an Outreach Program

a. Rules for assistance

b. Management (Personnel)

c. Operating Days

IX. Next meeting: February 15, 2002

X. Adjournment.

Note:The Agenda is a guide to keep the deliberating body on track. If adopted, it is to be followed loosely. For more flexibility, it may be adapted as a "guide only," thus leaving room to function more freely.

The fourth instrument, vital to ensure the church is staying on track, and to record decisions made, is Minutes. Here is a review of Minutes from the Board Agenda just presented.

MINUTES

Board of Directors/ Elders/ Business Deacons

January 16, 2002

1. Call to Order
   The meeting was called to order at 7:30 p.m. by Apostle Power at the local restaurant.
2. Prayer and Devotions
   The meeting was opened in prayer, led by John Hardworker. Bill Greatheart read from Hebrews 3:1-6 and offered some inspiring observations. Brief comments were also offered by several other members.
3. Roll Call
   Those present were Apostle Power, Bill Greatheart, John Hardworker, Steve Knight, James Less, and William Tell. Tom Early arrived late. Joe Sleeper was absent.
4. Agenda
   Motion prevailed to amend the proposed Agenda by deleting Article VIII, Section 2 concerning vehicle replacement, since all bids are not yet in. Motion prevailed to adopt the Agenda as amended.
5. Minutes
   The minutes were read from the regular meeting of December

10, and from the special meeting of December 20. Motion prevailed to approve the minutes as read. (Or, if there are no corrections, additions or deletions, let the minutes be approved as read). So let it be.

6. Old Business

   a. Three bids were submitted and discussed at length. Price, company reputation, and availability were the elements of prime concern. Motion prevailed to award the contract to The Alright Heating and Air Conditioning Company of Our Town in the amount of forty five thousand, two hundred and fifty dollars ($45,250), payable as follows:

   Five thousand dollars ($5,000) to be paid when the work is begun, and the balance upon completion. James Less and John Hardworker will see to satisfactory installation.

   b. Deacons – Though there has been significant growth in the congregation, it was determined that we should wait six months and reconsider the need then.

   c. John Doe Meetings – After lengthy discussion of timing, finances, etc., it was moved and seconded that John Doe be notified we will not proceed with the meetings at this time. The motion did not carry. Motion prevailed to invite John Doe to come to us for one week's meetings on a free-will basis the second full week of March. We are also to assure him that we will see that he is properly remunerated.

   d. Special Board Meetings – Due to the lateness of the hour and the importance of the rest of the Agenda, it was moved, seconded, and carried that we refer all unfinished business to a special meeting of this board to be held at the same place at 7 p.m. tomorrow.

   e. Adjournment or recess – The meeting was adjourned (recessed) at 9:15 p.m.

Importance of Minutes

A. They provide a permanent record of proceedings.

B. They are proof of your functioning as the Bylaws require.

C. They provide protection for people assigned certain duties, and present clear agreements regarding binding contracts, etc.

Filing Procedure

At least two copies of the Minutes should always be kept in the ministry office. One copy is to be placed in the regular file, in a file folder with the last meeting's Minutes filed in front. Another copy should be kept in the "minute book," (a loose leaf binder designated for this purpose) with the last meeting Minutes filed last. Please note that Minutes are to be filed by date.

Deacon and Congregation meeting Minutes may be kept separately in the regular file, but they are to be kept together in the "Minute Book" to provide continuity of action. For example, the Congregation Minutes of January 16, 2002. The docket will designate whether the action was Board or Congregation. Many times Deacon action must be ratified or otherwise coordinated with Congregation action. By this method of filing, the total picture is available with comparative ease. It may also be facilitated by cross reference.

Minutes

The Minutes are simply a record of the proceedings of the assembly, whether it be an assembly of the total membership or of some other governing body. Actions taken in such assemblies are binding upon the assembly providing they do not conflict with higher authority such as scripture, constitution, corporation articles, Bylaws of the parent organization, or the laws of the land. If the assembly wishes to do something which is in conflict with a higher document, such document must be amended according to its provision to accommodate such action before the action can be taken.

The Minuytes would reflect the assembly's action to amend any document but the amendment must take place according to the provisions of the document to be amended. Such records are of vital importance.

Articles of Faith

Each church has an inherent obligation to adopt a position on various questions of faith. Statements on some areas must be more specific than on others, but this need not be an elaborate theological treatise.

It does need to be treated sufficiently for a prospective member (or any member) to know what the church believes. A sample is provided on pages 137-145 of this book.

Articles of Incorporation

Although many churches are not incorporated, corporations are strongly encouraged. There are many advantages. The law of the land recognizes corporations as legal entities (literally as persons). A corporation stands upon its own right. It may sue or be sued in its own name. An incorporated church has more legal recognition than an unincorporated church and it is easier to own property and to do business in general through a corporation. It should also be noted that members and officers are not personally liable for claims against a corporation, providing all actions are taken in the name of the corporation and in accordance with its legal rights.

Articles of Incorporation are similar in content to the Constitution, but they are not necessarily identical. There should be a preliminary legal statement of the desire to incorporate, followed by:

I.   Name
II.   Place of Business
III.   Purpose
IV.   Officers (or Incorporators)
V.   Membership
VI.   Debts
VII.   Meetings
VIII.   Amendments
IX.   Dissolution Clause

Also, rights and authority of a corporation are only as provided in its Articles. Since corporations are creations of the State (at the request of a group of citizens), corporation requirements such as legal terminology may vary slightly from one state to another but the basic content of the

Articles as listed above does not generally change. Most states also require the appointment of an agent upon whom notice may be served. So, accompanying the proposed Articles, the corporation's agent must be listed along with his address. For a sample of a Constitution and Bylaws, please see the next section.

In the next section, you will find a Constitution and Bylaws which are suggested for consideration and adoption. A number of minor changes can be made to meet the needs of the individual church. For example, the amount of expenditures can be set by each church body, as can the number of Elders, etc. The terminology is a variable. Whatever term the church desires instead of "elder" may be substituted.

There is a supplement also enclosed which provides for both Ministering Elders and Business Elders if such organization is desired. By some re-arranging this can be substituted for certain sections of the Bylaws.

Some things are necessary in order to provide proper legal function and harmony with the parent organization. Be careful about deletions and substitutions. The Bylaws are more voluminous intentionally than the Constitution and are more easily amended. The Constitution should be kept brief, stating only the essentials of the organization - and allowing the rules and regulations to be included in the Bylaws.

Also, another Article may be added to the Bylaws which spells out "Standing Committees," such as assignments for individual leaders. One may be placed in charge of budget and finance, another in charge of building and grounds, another in charge of communion and ushers.

Another important document is the Articles of Incorporation. This is the document which makes the church a legal entity and spells out the purpose and powers of the church legally. Special attention should be given to it since the church can only do legally what this document authorizes.

Sample

C O N S T I T U T I O N

Vision Christian Church International

ARTICLE I

Section 1: NAME
> The name of this church shall be Vision Christian Church International.

Section 2: PLACE OF BUSINESS
> The principal place of business shall be (include complete address):
> 1115 D Street
> Ramona CA 92065

> or such other place as the membership or the Board of Elders may hereafter designate.

ARTICLE II

Section 1: PURPOSE
> The purpose of this organization shall be the propagation and dissemination of the gospel of Jesus Christ, through the preaching, teaching, and living of the gospel message as outlined in its Articles of Faith.

Section 2: AFFILIATION (if any)
> VCCI, having been affiliated with (organization) Churches, Inc. by means of a charter dated 2003 is, and shall be, an integral part of said (organization) Churches, Inc., and shall subscribe to its Articles of Faith.

ARTICLE III

Section 1: MEMBERSHIP

> There are two classes of membership: voting (Board) and non-voting (congregation). Voting members consist of the Director

58

of the Board of VCCI and the elected officers of the Board.

Non-voting Members

Membership in this church shall consist of those people twelve years of age and older who shall have been officially and publicly received into membership according to the Church Bylaws. Children under the age of twelve years, whose parents are members in good standing, shall be considered members of VCCI by filial relationship.

Section 2: VOTING

All active members of the Board in good standing and who have been members for at least thirty days shall have the right to vote in all regular and special called business meetings of the board membership.

Section 3: MEETINGS

There shall be an annual membership meeting held at a time and place designated by the membership and/or the board of elders in accordance with the Bylaws of VCCI for the purpose of conducting the business of the church. Special membership meetings may be called as provided for in the Bylaws.

ARTICLE IV

OFFICERS

The officers of this church shall consist of the Pastor, the Secretary, the Treasurer, a Board of seven (7) members, and such other officers as the membership and/or the elders shall determine from time to time. All these officers shall be twenty-one (21) years of age or older and shall be members in good standing. All officers of this church shall serve in accordance with the provisions of its Bylaws of VCCI, now in effect and as they may be amended from time to time, and fellowship with CRC Churches, International.

ARTICLE V

Section 1: CONSTITUTION AMENDMENTS

This Constitution may be amended by a two-thirds vote of the membership present at a regular or special-called meeting of the membership, providing the proposed amendment has been publicized to the church for a period of two weeks preceding the meeting.

Section 2: BYLAWS AMENDMENTS

The Bylaws may be amended by a majority vote of the membership present at any regular or special-called meeting of the membership, providing the proposed amendment has been publicized to the church for a period of two weeks preceding the meeting.

ARTICLE VI

DISSOLUTION

In the event that the ministry of VCCI is brought to a conclusion and this church is dissolved, all assets remaining after discharging all obligations and responsibilities of the church shall be turned over to CRC Churches, Inc., an (Australian) corporation, for disposition according to said corporation's policy for extinct churches. If said (organization) Churches is then non-existent, such assets shall be turned over to a religious, educational, or charitable organization or organizations whose objectives are in harmony with those of CRC Churches, Inc. Such recipient organization or organizations must also be exempt from Federal Income Taxation under the provisions of Section 501 (c) (3) of the Internal Revenue Code, or as such section may be amended. In no event may any of the assets of this church upon dissolution thereof be paid to or inure to the benefit of any individual member, director, or officer of this church, or any other private individual.

B Y L A W S

ARTICLE I

MEMBERSHIP – Non-Voting

Section 1: Admission

> Any person, twelve years of age or older, who has embraced the Christian Faith, experienced the New Birth, is in agreement with the Articles of Faith of this church and has agreed to work in harmony with the church's policies and leadership, shall be eligible for membership consideration.

> Applicants shall apply for membership on the form provided by the church and shall be examined by the Pastor or by another designated officer of the church. The examiner shall make a recommendation to the Board who shall take action on the application. The applicant shall be notified for membership, he or she shall be received publicly into membership according to the policy of the church.

Section 2: Privileges

> All active members in good standing shall have the rights and privileges normally given to the church members and/or as provided by the church policy as it shall be amended from time to time. All such members who are eighteen (18) years of age or older and who have been members for at least thirty (30) days shall have the right to be heard in all regular and special membership business meetings.

Section 3: Filial Relationship

> Children under the age of twelve (12) years whose parents (or parent) are members in good standing shall be considered members of VCCI by filial relationship.

Section 4: Voting Members

Voting members consist of the Board of Directors (7), Pastor, Secretary, and Treasurer of the Corporation.

ARTICLE II

OFFICERS (Voting members)

Section 1: Enumerated

The officers of this church shall consist of the Pastor, the Secretary, the Treasurer, a board of seven (7) Elders, and such other officers as the membership and/or the board of directors shall determine from time to time. All officers shall be twenty-one (21) years of age or older.

Section 2: Pastor

The Pastor must be a credentialed minister in good standing with Vision Christian Church International. He is appointed by a two thirds (2/3) majority of the membership present at a meeting duly called for that purpose. The initial term shall be indefinite.

The Pastor shall be chairman of the board of directors and shall call to order all meetings of that board and the regular membership (non-voting) meetings. He may also call a special membership meeting.

The pastor shall be the spiritual and temporal leader of the church and shall minister to the spiritual needs of the people, guard the membership against dissension and put forth his best efforts for the promulgation and dissemination of the full gospel message as set forth in the Articles of Faith. He shall strive consistently for the up-building of Christian Life in the membership and in the community.

The pastor shall have full responsibility in the supervision of all the services and ministries of the church and all meetings of the church membership and officials except as otherwise herein provided, and shall have general supervision over all departments such as Sunday School, Youth, Music, Missions, Fellowship Groups, etc. He shall be ex-officio member of all church bodies and organizations.

Section 3: Secretary

The Secretary shall be appointed by the Pastor with the approval of the Board of Elders. His term of office shall be until the next annual membership meeting. He shall be chosen from the Board of Elders.

The Secretary shall keep a true and accurate account of all membership business meetings and all business meetings of the board of elders. He shall serve as Secretary of the Board of Elders and as Secretary of any other body or committee of the church as desired by the Pastor. He shall submit to the Pastor and to the board of elders an annual report of his office, showing all transactions therein, and he shall, when required by the Pastor or by an authorized officer of VCCI submit special reports and furnish special data. He shall, under the direction of the Pastor, provide for the safekeeping of all records and documents of the church.

In addition to the duties herein described, he shall perform all other duties as are consistent with his office, and such as may, from time to time, be required of him by the Pastor, the Board of Directors, or an authorized officer of VCCI.

Section 4: Treasurer

A. The Treasurer shall be appointed by the pastor with the approval of the Board of Directors. His term of office shall be until the next annual membership meeting. He shall not be a member of the Board of Directors.
B. The Treasurer shall keep an itemized accounting of all receipts and disbursements of monies committed to his trust in a proper and businesslike manner.

1) He shall make monthly reports to the Board of Directors, and upon request, he shall make reports to the membership, pastor, and authorized officers of VCCI.

2) His books shall be open for inspection at any time to the Pastor, the Board of Directors, or an authorized officer of VCCI.

3) He shall submit a report of the finances to the church at the annual membership meeting.

C. The Treasurer shall manage the funds as a good steward under the supervision of the Board of Elders. Funds shall be deposited with a reputable institution in such a way as to require two (2) signatures for withdrawal.

D. The Treasurer shall, by virtue of his office, be a member of the Finance Committee.

Section 5: Board of Directors, Overseers

The Board of Directors shall consist of seven (7) members who shall be elected by a majority vote of the membership[8] present at the annual business meeting. The term of office for a Director shall be for three (3) years. No Director shall serve longer than two (2) consecutive terms. However, one may serve again after an absence of one year from the Board.

The initial election in VCCI will be for seven (7) Elders of which two (2) will be elected for one (1) year terms, two (2) for two (2) year terms, and three (3) for three (3) year terms. Thereafter, all terms shall be for a period of three (3) years.

The Board of Directors shall be the advisory body of the church, and shall attend to the business thereof, except those duties specifically designated to the membership or to another officer. They shall assist the Pastor in the program of the church and see that all financial obligations are met as they become due. The Board of Directors shall serve as Directors and Trustees of the church properties. The Directors shall determine the salary and/or offerings for the Pastor and for all other employees of the church with assistance from the Apostolic Council. They shall be leaders of the church body

---

[8] Note: Remember, membership is key leaders.

and shall work with the Pastor to promote maximum spiritual growth and unity. They shall be examples of Christian character and practices including discipline in their own lives, in their homes, and in the church. For Biblical guidelines on qualifications and for church officers, see I Timothy 3: 1-13 and Titus 1:5.

The Board of Directors shall, at their first meeting following the election, choose one of their number to serve as vice-chairman of the Board until the next annual membership meeting. The vice-chairman shall preside over all meetings of said Board when the Pastor is absent.

ARTICLE III

ELECTIONS

Section 1: Nominating Committee

> The officers of the church except the Pastor, Secretary, and Treasurer shall be on the nominating committee consisting of three (3) members of the present Board of Directors and the Pastor who shall be the chairman of the committee. The slate of nominees shall be presented to the Board of Directors for approval and then to the membership for consideration.

Section 2: Tellers

> Tellers for handling the ballots shall be appointed by the presiding officer of the meeting. The number shall be three (3) or more as the need requires. The chairman of the Tellers shall be a member of the Board of Business Directors. The others shall be chosen from the membership.

Section 3: Election Method

> Elections shall be only by secret ballot. Officers are elected by a two-thirds (2/3) majority vote of the members present at the meeting.

ARTICLE IV

VACANCIES

Section 1: Pastor/Apostle

> When a vacancy occurs in the office of Pastor, the Board of Directors shall notify the Apostolic Council. One of them will meet with the board of elders and discuss possible available persons to fill the vacancy. The Board of Directors shall choose the order in which candidates are to be considered. When a candidate is considered, he shall minister to the church on a Sunday (longer if desired) and the membership shall vote the following Sunday meeting whether to extend a pastoral call. If two-thirds (2/3) majority affirmative vote is received, the candidate receives the call, the vacancy is filled, and no other candidates are considered. If such vote is not received, the candidate is notified and the next candidate is considered, etc., etc.

Section 2: Secretary, Treasurer, Directors

In case a vacancy occurs in the office of Secretary or Treasurer, or on the Board of Directors before the expiration of the term involved, the Pastor may appoint a successor to fill the unexpired term, subject to the approval of the Board of Directors.

ARTICLE V

RECORDS

Section 1: Membership (Non-voting)

> Adequate membership records shall be maintained at all times. They shall have the following four (4) categories: Active, Inactive, Deceased, and Removed.
>
> 1) The Active category shall include all members not transferred to another category. Active members shall have the right of voice.
> 2) The Inactive category shall include any member who shall

absent himself from the church services without just cause for a period of ninety (90) days and/or shall withhold his financial support for the same period of time. Inactive members shall not have the right of voice or vote in the church business meetings.

3) The Deceased category shall be a permanent record of deceased members. The Pastor or Secretary shall duly mark and transfer such names upon receipt of proof of death.

4) The Removed category shall consist of those persons whose names are removed by action of the Board of Directors in session because the member has moved away and contact is lost, or because the member has joined another church, or because there is reason to believe the member's life is not consistent with wholesome Christian Living and a fair hearing has been offered, or because the member no longer adheres to the doctrines and policies of the church, or because the member terminates membership voluntarily.

Section 2: Records (other)

Orderly permanent records shall be kept in the church files of all marriages, dedications, baptisms, and funerals held in the church and/or by a church officer on the church's behalf. The exception shall be if the facilities are let to those outside the church body for any of these services, the church shall not be responsible for such records.

ARTICLE VI

BUSINESS MEETINGS

Section 1: Board of Directors

The Board of Directors shall hold regular monthly meetings in the interest of the church program and business. A majority of the members of the Board of Directors present at such duly called meetings shall constitute a quorum thereof for the transaction of business.

The pastor may call special meetings of the Board of Directors when he deems it is advisable to do so.

Section 2: Membership

There shall be an annual meeting of the membership (voting and non-voting) for the purpose of transacting church business. It shall be held at the church address on the evening of the mid-week meeting in the third (3rd) week of May. (arbitrary date)

Special membership meetings may be called by the pastor. Such membership meetings for the purpose of determining policy or resolving important issues shall require two (2) weeks notice. Membership meetings for the purpose of polling non-voting members for their opinions or for consultation may be called on shorter notice. When there are no extenuating circumstances requiring otherwise, the purpose of the meeting shall be started. Any percentage of the active members present at such duly called meetings shall constitute a quorum.

Section 3: Procedure

1) Order. Business meetings shall be conducted according to Roberts Rules of Order and the Policies and Principles of VCCI. Confirmed actions recorded in the membership minutes shall also constitute church policy and procedure.

2) Agenda (Suggested)

   a. Devotions
   b. Reading of minutes from previous meeting
   c. Reports (Officers, Committees, etc...)
   d. Unfinished business
   e. Other business
   f. Adjournment
   g. Prayer

ARTICLE VII

DISMISSAL

Section 1: Leaders

When a leader of the church falls into a spiritual condition that makes such leader a detriment to his or her office or diminishes his or her effectiveness for good, the pastor shall then have the authority and right to remove him or her from office after proper consultation with the one in question.

When such leader is an officer of the church, the pastor shall have the right of dismissal after consultation with the board of directors and by advisement of the Apostolic Council.

Section 2: Membership

A member may be removed from membership upon the pastor's recommendation by action of the board of elders in session, providing however, if there are charges against the member, such member has been given the right to be heard.

ARTICLE VIII

DEPARTMENT HEADS

Department heads of the church shall be appointed by the Pastor with the approval of the Board of Directors.

ARTICLE IX

FINANCES

Section 1: Income

The church operation shall be financed by the tithes and offerings of its members and friends and by projects approved by the Board of Directors.

Section 2: Expenditures

In order to maintain a true Christian testimony the church shall always stay current in its financial obligations. No expense above $1,000.00 shall be incurred without the approval of the Board of Directors and no expense above $10,000.00 shall be incurred without the approval of the membership.

ARTICLE X

PROPERTIES

Section 1: Right to Own

> The church shall have the right to purchase, through its officers, and to own, real properties and whatever channels it deems advisable in promotion of its purpose.

Section 2: Right to Sell

> The church shall have the right to mortgage, sell, or to otherwise dispose of any of its various properties through its officers, in the furtherance of its purpose. However, no real properties may be mortgaged, sold, or otherwise alienated or encumbered without a majority approval of the membership.

ARTICLE XI

OFFICERS EMPOWERED TO ACT

The Chairman of the Board of Directors and the Secretary of the corporation shall sign and execute all legal documents of every kind and nature, which shall be binding upon said corporation, upon appropriate resolution made and entered by the board of directors, or the membership, of said corporation.

However, in the matter of authority for the withdrawal and/or expenditure of funds, the directors, in session, shall have the power to name one (1) or two (2) additional officers and provide that any two (2) or the four (4) officers so designated thereby shall have the power to act.

ARTICLE XII

APOSTOLIC COUNCIL

The pastor shall have an Apostolic Council (may consist of denominational leadership) who shall act as overseers of the Pastor, Counsel, advisor, and shall, upon approval of the Board, act as arbitrators in times of conflict, assist in pastoral search, etc. The Council shall consist of a minimum of three and maximum of five Senior leaders, chosen by the Pastor, to serve at the will of the Pastor and Board.

ARTICLE XIII

AMENDMENT

These Bylaws may be amended by a majority vote of the membership at any duly called membership meeting, providing however, the amendment has been publicized to the membership two (2) weeks before such meeting.

BYLAWS: ARTICLE II SUBSTITUTE (Alternate)

Section 5: Oversight

There shall be two groups of Directors: Business Directors and Ministerial Directors.

A. General Requirements
In order to serve God more effectively in the directorship of the church, it is necessary that an individual have a proper relationship to God, the church, the family, self, and to the world. Therefore, it is incumbent upon such officers to meet the following qualifications:

1. One must be a Christian believer, in harmony with the church and of good report from without.
2. Be a member of VCCI in good standing, and
3. Have attained a degree of Christian maturity worthy of his assignment.
4. He must support the church with his prayers, presence, and material substance faithfully, and
5. Be part of the leadership team (Not quarrelsome and independent but capable of both leadership in the church and to be subject to fellow officers), and

6. Have capabilities for proficiency in the area of service designated. Business Directors see to the management of church business according to the policies of VCCI church. Ministry Directors shall be able to teach and otherwise serve the church in personal ministry.

7. One must meet Biblical requirements as stated for such office in I Timothy 3, including control of himself and his household.

B. Business Directors

The Board of Business Directors shall consist of seven (7) members who shall be elected by a majority vote of the membership present at the annual meeting, or at a meeting duly called for that purpose.

The term of office shall be for a period of three (3) years. No Director shall serve longer than two (2) consecutive terms. He may serve again after a year of absence from the board.

The Board of Business Directors shall be the advisory body of the church and shall attend to the business thereof, except those duties specifically designated otherwise. The Board of Business Directors shall assist the Pastor in the program of the church and shall see that all obligations are met as they become due. The Boards of Business Directors shall be the Board of Directors and Trustees of the church properties. It shall determine the salary or offering to be given the Pastor and all employees. The Treasurer shall see that this arrangement is carried out.

The Board of Business Directors shall work with the Pastor to promote maximum spiritual growth and unity. Its members shall be examples of Christian character and practices, including discipline in their own lives as becomes Christian Believers. For Biblical statements on qualifications for church officers see I Timothy 3: 1-13 and Titus 1: 5-9.

The Board of Business Directors shall, at their first meeting following the annual membership meeting, elect one of their number to act as Vice-chairman of the Board. The Vice-chairman shall preside over all meetings of the Board in the absence of the Pastor.

C. Ministering Directors

Ministering Directors shall be chosen by the Holy Spirit and appointed to office by the Senior Pastor in consultation with the Board of Business Directors.

All persons holding pastoral posts shall, by virtue of such office, be members of the Body of Ministering Directors. Ministering Directors shall serve a one (1) year term, except the Senior Pastor whose term is described elsewhere. However, members of the pastoral staff shall not be subject to the three (3) term limitation specified below.

There shall be a number, up to seven (7), chosen from the church membership as the need requires, excluding the pastoral staff. They shall be appointed to their posts as herein provided and shall work under the direction of the Senior Pastor. There shall be a regular monthly meeting. Other meetings are subject to call by the Senior Pastor when desirable.

No member can serve more than three (3) consecutive terms. After a period of one year's absence from office, he may be appointed again for up to three (3) consecutive terms.

The purpose of such office is to take the oversight of areas of ministry as assigned by the Senior Pastor and to assist him in such ways as are feasible and desired. This shall include (but not necessarily be limited to) ministry to shut-ins, spiritual counseling with members of the congregation, admonishing and encouraging the membership, and working in general for the church's well being.

The Ministerial Directors shall, at their first meeting following the annual membership meeting, choose a Vice-chairman of the group. The Vice-chairman shall preside over all meetings of the group in the absence of the Senior Pastor.

Specific responsibilities shall be reviewed from time to time and changed when profitable to the church and its ministries.

NOTE: If the following is desired as a part of the Bylaws it is recommended that it be inserted as Article VIII and the succeeding Articles numbered in sequence.

ARTICLE IX

STANDING COMMITTEES

There shall be standing committees as follows:

Section 1: Communion

> The purpose of the Communion Committee shall be to serve the symbols of the "Lord's Supper" according to the policy of the church. The number of members shall be commensurate with the need. The members shall be chosen by the Ministerial Directors and the Chairman, who shall be responsible for the preparation of the symbols, shall be a member of the Ministerial Directors.

Section 2: Finance and Development

> A. There shall be a Finance Committee which shall be responsible for the receipt and disbursement of the funds of the church and for developing and recommending and operating budget to the Board of Business Directors.

> 1. This committee shall be composed of a chairman who shall be chosen from the Board of Business Directors, the Vice-chairman of the Board of Business Directors,

the Treasurer of the church, and two (2) additional members appointed by the Pastor with the approval of the Board of Business Directors. The appointment shall be made at the first meeting of the Board of Business Directors following the annual membership meeting. The term of office for each member shall be one (1) year with the right of succession if reappointed.

2. The Finance Committee shall make monthly reports to the Board of Business Directors.

B. The Finance Committee shall authorize expenditures only upon approval of the Board of Business Directors except in matters of emergency requiring attention before the next meeting of the Board of Business Directors and such expenditure shall not exceed the limit prescribed in Article IX, Section 2.

C. All monies received from offerings and all other sources shall be deposited by the treasurer in a bank designated by the Finance Committee. Two (2) signatures shall be required for the withdrawal of funds from any accounts.

D. There shall be a Department of Development, consisting of not more than seven (7) members which shall serve under the direction of the Finance Committee. Its members shall be appointed by the Finance Committee for a term of one (1) year with the right of succession if reappointed. Such appointments are to be approved by the Board of Business Directors. Services that are to be provided by the department, as desired by members and friends of the church are:

1. To provide sound investment opportunities for the assistance of ministries of Vision Christian Church International and to provide for prompt return of the investment to the investor when requested. Individual investment plans of varied maturities and income arrangements are to be offered, and,

2. To plan the investment of gifts and memorials.

E. All decisions of this department shall be in compliance with the laws of the land and Bylaws of Vision Christian Church International. The execution of said responsibilities shall be final.

F. The Finance Committee shall supervise the fiscal management of all church ministries authorized by the Board of Business Directors. Separate banking accounts shall be maintained as determined advisable. These ministries, whether a part of Vision Christian Church International corporation or a subsidiary corporation, shall submit monthly financial reports to the Finance Committee. Also, annual operating statements and statements of assets and liabilities shall be submitted at the end of each calendar year.

Section 3: Ushers

Ushers shall be chosen by the Ministering Directors, and the Ushers Committee chairman shall be a member of the Ministerial Directors appointed by the Pastor. Terms of office shall be for one (1) year with the right of succession if reappointed.

Section 4: Building and Grounds

A member of the Board of Business Directors shall be chosen by that Board as overseer of the buildings and grounds owned by Vision Christian Church International. His term of office shall be for one (1) year with the right of succession if reappointed. He shall choose other members of his committee each year as he deems advisable, with the approval of the Board of Business Elders.

Section 5: Outreach

The Ministering Directors shall choose one of their number as Chairman of the Outreach Committee. His term of office shall be for one (1) year with the right of succession if reappointed. He shall choose other members of his committee each year as he deems advisable with the approval of the Ministering Directors.

This Committee shall have the oversight of:
1) Christian Education,
2) Visitation, and
3) Missions -- Home and Foreign.

Section 6: Planning

The Board of Business Directors shall choose one of their number as chairman of the Planning Committee. His term of office shall be for a period of one (1) year with the right of succession if reappointed. He shall choose other members of his committee each year as he deems advisable with the approval of the Board of Business Directors.

"Management is known by the company it keeps."

- Anonymous

CHAPTER 6

MANAGING RECORDS

Without adequate records, the church is hampered in its progress. Without a clear knowledge of our history we may end up almost anywhere. How we arrived at where we are and to help determine our direction from here, we need a concise picture of our past. Each area of records has its own value, as we will see in the course of this section.

We will discuss church records in two basic categories: (1) Filing and (2) Bookkeeping. These will be covered in a general way, so to be adequate with as little detail as possible. Since church business involves many legal matters, it is imperative to have accurate records.

Filing

Filing is said to be the "memory" of business. It has to do with one of the most important assets of an organization - its records. It is the process of classifying and arranging records so that they will be kept safely and will be obtainable when needed.

1. Who Needs Files?

All people in places of leadership and responsibility need files. Of course, adequate membership files must be kept by a ministry. This may be done through a membership book, by a card system, or through various computer systems. The latter is preferred, if one is computer literate. However, until one is computer savvy, hard copy systems will do. The assumption of this book is that you are technologically challenged or you do not have computer programs available to you.

The Pastor should have an adequate up-to-date address file on each family who attends the church. A card file is recommended, which includes telephone numbers and, if married, the spouse's name and names and birth dates of the children, if any. It should be convenient to the Pastor's desk and the secretary should have a duplicate file (if you have a secretary).

Department heads and class teachers should have similar files on the people to whom they minister.

2. What Kinds of Records are Kept?

People

Membership, baptism, marriages, and funerals are to be recorded and kept permanently. Membership records are in four categories: Active, Inactive, Deceased and Removed.

Minutes

Membership meetings and board meetings should be retained permanently.

Valued Papers

Contracts, agreements, leases, insurance policies, deeds, bonds, notes-receivable and payable, checkbooks, bank statements and cancelled checks, interest coupons, paid and unpaid, should be kept up to ten years.

Financial

Internal Revenue Service information and data should be kept for five years after due date. Employee payroll records are to be kept permanently. Financial reports, journals, and ledgers are to be kept permanently. Invoices paid and receipts for disbursements should be kept on file for five years after payment.

3. Methods of Filing

There are two basic methods of filing: alphabetic and numeric. Because of limited time and the nature of our purpose, we will confine our studies to the alphabetic method. It simply means filing according to the sequence of the alphabet.

Two terms are used: unit and indexing. A unit is any part of a name that is compared separately with other parts of other names to determine filing arrangement. In the name John Brown Company, there are three units-John, Brown and Company. In the name Joseph LaZaro there are two units- Joseph and LaZaro - because the La is not considered separately.

Indexing means to determine the order in which to consider the units of a name. In John Brown Company, which of the three units should be compared first, second, and third with the units of other names? In Joseph LaZaro, which of the two units is to be considered first and second?

4. Alphabetic Filing Rules

Because it is the purpose of the basic rules of filing to help determine units and the order in which those units should be considered, they are often referred to as "Indexing and Filing" rules.

a. Names of Individuals

Transpose the names of individuals. Consider the surname (last name) first, the given name (first name) second and the middle name, if any, third.

Example:

NAME	FILING ARRANGEMENT
Stan E. DeKoven	DeKoven, Stan E.
G. Randolph Gurley	Gurley, G. Randolph
Maureen Kelley	Kelley, Maureen

b. Alphabetic Order:

Each word in the name is an indexing unit. Arrange the names in alphabetic order by comparing similar units in each name. Consider the second units only when the first units are identical. Consider the third units only when both the first and second units are identical.

Example:

NAME	FILING ARRANGEMENT
DeKoven	DeKoven
Stan DeKoven	DeKoven, Stan
S. DeKoven	DeKoven, S.
Maureen Kelley	Kelley, Maureen

c. Surname Prefixes:

A surnames prefix is not a separate indexing unit, but is considered part of the surname. These prefixes include: d', D', Da, de, De, Del, Des, Di, Du, Fitz, La, Le, M', Mac, Mc, O', St, Van, Van der, Von, Von der, and others. The prefixes M' and Mac, and Mc are indexed and filed as though spelled out.

Example:

NAME	FILING ARRANGEMENT
Stan DeKoven	DeKoven, Stan

d. Names of Firms

Names of firms and institutions are indexed and filed exactly as they are written when they do not contain the complete name of an individual.

Example:

NAME	FILING ARRANGEMENT
Center Grocery Company	Center Grocery Company
Curtis Secretarial School	Curtis Secretarial School

e. Names of Firms Containing Complete Individual Names:

When the firm or institution includes the complete name of an individual, the units are transposed for indexing in the same way as the name of an individual.

Example:

NAME	FILING ARRANGEMENT
John Drew Lumber Co.	Drew, John Lumber Co.
Arthur Miller Corp.	Miller, Arthur Corp.

f. Article "The"

When "The" occurs at the beginning of a name, it is placed at the end in parentheses when writing names on cards and folders; if in the middle, it is placed in parentheses but is not moved.

Example:

NAME	FILING ARRANGEMENT
Harry the Tailor	Harry (The) Tailor
The Allen Tailor Corp.	Tailor, Allen Corp. (The)
The Tailor Dairy	Tailor, Dairy (The)

g. Hyphenated Names

Hyphenated firm names are considered as separate units. Hyphenated surnames of individuals are considered as one indexing unit: this applies also to hyphenated names of individuals whose complete names are part of the firm name.

Example:

NAME	FILING ARRANGEMENT
Lee-Barry Garage	Lee-Barry Garage
John Lee-Barry	Lee-Barry, John
The John Lee-Barry Co.	Lee-Barry, John Co. (The)

h. Abbreviations

Abbreviations are considered as though the names were written in full; however, single letters other than abbreviations are considered as separate indexing units.

Example:

NAME	FILING ARRANGEMENT
ABC Products	ABC Products
Chas. Atlas	Atlas, Charles
CIT Corp.	CIT Corporation
St. George Hotel	Saint George Hotel

i. Bank Names

Because the names of many banking institutions are alike in several respects, as First National Bank, Second National Bank, etc. banks are indexed and filed first by city location, then by bank name, with the state location written on a card or a folder in parentheses and considered only if necessary.

Example:

NAME   FILING ARRANGEMENT
First National Bank of Miami   Miami, First National Bank
First National Bank of Mobile, Alabama   Mobile, First National Bank

j. Married Women

The legal name of a married woman is the one used for filing purposes. Legally, a man's surname is the only part of a man's name a woman assumes when she married. Her legal name, therefore, could be either:

1. Her own first and middle names together with her husband's surname, or,
2. Her own first name and maiden surname together with her husband's surname. Mrs. is placed in parentheses after the names when written on a card or folder. Her husband's first and middle names are given in parentheses below her legal name.

Example:

NAME   FILING ARRANGEMENT
Mrs. Robert C. Eagan   Eagan, Helen Ann (Mrs.)
(Helen Ann)   (Robert C.)

5. Steps in the filing process:

a. Inspecting

Inspect each piece to make sure it has been released for filing. Has it been approved, answered and initialed by the various persons or departments who should have seen it?

b. Indexing

Determine the name, subject or other caption under which it should be filed. (Use the most likely heading under which correspondence will be requested from file.) When a paper might be called for in several ways, it is filed under the most important caption and cross-referencing means placing a sheet of paper containing information about the actual location of a document in all places in the file where a person might look for that document. Cross-reference sheets are usually a distinctive color.

c. Filing

When actually placing papers or records in a file, a predetermined plan should be used. All papers, regardless of size, are placed in the folders with the headings to the left as you face the file. The most recent date is placed in front. Never overcrowd folders. They have a maximum capacity of 100 sheets of paper. It is best to subdivide papers before reaching this capacity.

6. Filing Materials and Their Use

a. Guides

Guides perform two functions: (1) they act as "signposts", i.e., they guide the eye quickly to the place desired in the drawer, (2) they help to support the records contained in the drawer. The most commonly used are 1/5th or 1/3rd cuts. One-fifth cut gives you five positions across the file and one-third cut gives you only three.

b. Folders

File folders are available in a variety of styles and materials. The amount and kind of materials to be filed, and the type and extent of handling should determine your selection. For ordinary use, manila folders are recommended. They are available in different weights and cuts. You can have them with straight edges or with tabs of various positions.

c. Filing Cabinets

Filing cabinets, like file folders, should be chosen with consideration for the materials they will contain. It is best to choose a locking file, and if possible, a fireproof one. However, the fireproof file is more expensive. If there is a safe available, valuable papers such as insurance policies, contracts, mortgages, bonds, checkbooks, etc. should, by all means, be kept there. If not, a locking fireproof file will suffice.

d. Tickler File

A tickler file is basically a memorandum or follow-up file. It may be arranged in many forms and may be used for memos of all types. An expando type folder with twelve pockets is a good beginning. Label them, January through December. Memos on things to be done throughout the year are placed in the proper month: mortgage payments, insurance premiums, property tax, etc. This is an aid to meeting deadlines on certain obligations and duties. For example, you have a mortgage payment on the 6th day of each month. A memo card or sheet of paper is made of that payment and placed in the proper month, say January. On January 1st, you will check your tickler file. Pull out the memo, prepare the payment and place the memo in the "February" pocket. All kinds of materials can be handled in this way without as many "slip-ups" on important items.

Treat your office procedures as though you were handling the most important business in the world --- for INDEED YOU ARE!!!

"In filling out an income tax return, let an accountant instead of your conscience by your guide."

- Will Rogers

CHAPTER 7

BOOKKEEPING

The financial records of the church include receipts and disbursements as well as the source of income and the purpose of expenditures. Honesty, confidentiality, integrity, accuracy and consistency are essential characteristics of a good bookkeeper.

1. Basic Rules

The treasurer of an organization acts in a responsible fiduciary capacity. He must keep in mind that an auditor normally will be reviewing his work and an "audit trail" must be left by the treasurer for the auditor to follow. While the treasurer may now know who, what, why, when and where, will he know all this information two or three years from now and will someone else be able to follow the transactions? The treasurer must be above reproach at all times. Remember, ignorance of the rules is certainly no excuse for failure to perform properly. A few basic rules are listed below.

a. Cash Receipts

All cash receipts should be deposited, intact, in a bank account as soon as possible after their receipt and a record of the source and date of receipt should be recorded in the cash receipts journal. The person, or persons, who make deposits or handle cash receipts should not be authorized to sign checks.

b. Cash Disbursements

All cash disbursements should be made by check with proper supporting evidence as to the propriety of the disbursement. Examples of proper supporting evidence are invoices, requisitions, vouchers and/or authorization by duly constituted persons or a group of persons. Statements from venders or suppliers that cover a period of time are not normally proper support. Each invoice should have the date paid and check number written on it and filed. If there is no invoice, a plain sheet of paper with an explanation as to what is being paid and the authority for payment will suffice. To prevent the loss of cash register tapes and other small invoices, it is recommended that they be stapled to a larger sheet of paper before filing.

c. Statements and Reports

Periodic statements and/or reports should be made to the officers, owners, membership, etc. A qualified accountant should establish the proper form and type of statements for your church. The controlling parties should establish the frequency of such reports.

d. Bank Reconciliation

The checking account should be reconciled monthly and all cancelled checks retained; also, the bank statement. (If you do not know how to reconcile a bank account, obtain help!)

e. Journals

A cash-receipts and cash-disbursements journal should be maintained in all cases, summarizing the transactions described in a and b previously listed. As each organization is different, the journal should be specially designed for the organization by a qualified accountant. (Note: A bookkeeper is not necessarily an accountant) Ledgers should be used as needed.

f. Audits

There are two types of audits for non-governmental types of organization, internal audits and independent audits. Internal audits are performed by someone within the organization and independent audits are performed by Certified Public Accountants. Needless to say, each organization should be audited periodically by one of the above types.

If you are negligent or slothful you do your church a great injustice to accept the position of treasurer. Such a position requires strong Christian character and a conscientious dedication to a very honorable task.

2. Procedures for Church Financial Record Keeping[9]

a. Receipts:

1) Offerings received are entered in the Ushers cash book and given to the bookkeeper along with any information received - envelopes, notations, etc.
2) All funds received, including those received by mail, etc. are entered in the cash receipts journal by the bookkeeper.
3) The deposit is then prepared for banking and must agree with the total cash receipts representing this deposit. The deposit is then made to the bank and the bank receipt attached to the duplicate copy of the deposit slip and filed in the church office. The record of the deposit is then entered on the checkbook stub showing the date and amount of the deposit and is reflected in the checkbook balance.
4) Post each entry shown in the journal to the General Ledger (Receipts) both in the cash column and in the proper account column. Use a small check mark (/) to show you have posted each item. Show cash receipts journal page (Crj-1) from which the item was posted.
5) Post contributions to individual contributions ledger (card, sheet, book, etc.)

b. Disbursements

Pay all bills by check.

1) Prepare the check showing name, amount, date and description such as invoice #, salary through (date), utilities, etc. Duplicate this information on the check stub.
2) Enter each disbursement in the cash disbursements journal, showing check #, to whom paid, and for what purpose the check was written.
3) POST to the General Ledger (Disbursements) in the cash column and in the proper account column. Show cash disbursements

---

[9] There are several organizations which specialize in financial and corporate records management. Some are listed in the back of this book, and must be evaluated by the church leadership.

journal page (Cdj-1) from which the item was posted. Use small check mark (/) to show you have posted each item.

Note: if a cash disbursements journal is not used, the check number must show on the General Ledger disbursement entry.

c. Closing the General Ledgers

At the end of each month, draw a single red line after your last entry. (If there are adjusting entries the line is drawn after the last adjusting entry.) Total all columns. Use a pencil footing in small figures until all columns are in balance. When the amount of the CASH column is equal to the amount of all the following columns combined, the ledger is said to be in balance. You will then enter the totals in ink and draw a double red line under them. This means the ledger is now closed for that month.

d. Financial Reports and Statements

At the end of each month (or accounting period) the totals from the General Ledgers are organized in report form (see Appendix 4). The receipts and disbursements are shown by categories and the balance is shown. This gives a clear picture of your financial status. At least one copy is filed in the church office files and one more copy is submitted to the Board of Directors. An annual report is usually submitted to the church membership.

BUDGET BOOK SIMPLIFIED

MONTHLY EXPENDITURES				by Check, Cash, or Visa	
Date	To Whom Paid	Check No.	Acct. No.	Amount	
MONTHLY TOTAL					

MONTH OF _____, 200__

Acct. No.	Income Received	Total		Budget for the Month	Over + Short -	
	#1 Tithe					
	#2 Donation					
	#3 other income					
	TOTAL INCOME					
1	Accounting					
2	Auto Exp.					
3	Electricity/Gas					
4	Education					
5	Food/Beverages					
6	Donations					
7	Health Insurance					
8	Liability Insurance					
9	Renters/Owners Insurance					
10	Misc. Exp.					
11	Postage/Shipping					
12	Repairs					
13	Rent/Mortgage					
14	Telephone					
15	Office Supplies					
16	Development					
17	Savings					
18	Technology					
19	Payroll					

TAX DEDUCTIBLE						
20	Church/Contrib.					
21	Tax					
22						
23						
24						
25						
	TOTAL SPENDING					

NARRATIVE OF TRANSACTIONS FOR JANUARY, _____

Receipts:

DATE	MONEY
January 7	Sunday morning offering = $150.00 $25.00 went to the building fund and $125.00 to the general fund. Sunday evening offering = $75.00 to the general fund.
January 10	Wednesday evening offering to the general fund.
January 14	Sunday morning offering $225.00. $125.00 went to the general fund and $100.00 was for World Evangelism. Sunday evening offering $60.00. $50.00 for general fund and $10.00 for the Youth Dept.
January 17	Wednesday evening offering, $15.00 for the general fund.
January 28	Sunday morning offering $300.00. $200.00 went to the general fund and $100.00 went to the building fund. Sunday evening offering $150.00 was designated for the special speaker. (Designate Unclassified).
January 31	Wednesday evening offering $15.00 for the general fund.

Disbursements:

January 1	Minister's salary through January 15, $200.00 (General Fund) _____Churches, Inc. $68.75. Of this amount $18.75 was for _____plan and $50.00 was for World Evangelism.
January 15	Blank Power and Light Company – church utilities $25.00 (General Fund). Minister's salary through January 31, $200.00 (General Fund)
January 28	Special Speaker (William Smith) to be paid the amount of $150.00 (Unclassified).
January 30	Roth Office Supply $5.00 (General Fund).

Total Receipts of the month should be $1, 025.00

Total Disbursements for the month should be $648.75

CASH DISBURSEMENTS JOURNAL

Date		Description		Chk#\Postref\Act Pbl.\Cash-Credit						

CASH DISBURSEMENTS JOURNAL

Date	Description		Chk#\Postref\Act Pbl.\Cash-Credit						

Church_____

Cash Receipts Journal

Date	Description	Post Ref	Receipts	Deposits

CHURCH_____

City, State

Financial Report

January 31, 2002

Balance, January 1, 2002 $1000.00

Cash Receipts for January:

General Fund

General Offerings $630.00

Special Speaker $150.00 $780.00

World Evangelism:

Offerings, Faith Promises $100.00 $100.00

Christian Education:

Youth Offerings $10.00 $10.00

Building Fund:

Contributions $135.00 $135.00

Total Cash Receipts

     $1,025.00

Total $2,025.00

Disbursements:

<u>General Fund</u>:

Salaries	$400.00	
Flowers	$18.75	
Special Speaker	$150.00	
Office Supplies	$5.00	
Utilities, church	$25.00	$598.75

<u>World Evangelism</u>:

December Offerings	$50.00	$50.00

Total Cash Disbursements

   <u>$648.75</u>

Balance, January 31, 2002

   <u>$1,376.25</u>

Balance by Departments:

General Fund	$681.00
World Evangelism	$100.00
Christian Education	$60.00
Building Fund	<u>$535.00</u>
Balance, January 31, 2002	<u>$1,376.25</u>

<u>NOTE</u>: Old-balance by departments shown here for clarification only, they would not be shown on each monthly statement or report.

Balance by Departments: (December 31, 2001)

General Fund	$500.00
World Evangelism	$50.00
Christian Education	$50.00
Building Fund	$400.00
Balance, December 31, 2001	$1,000.00

"To accomplish something important, two things are necessary: a definite idea, and not quite enough time."

- Anonymous

CHAPTER 8

PROMOTION OF MINISTRY THROUGH POLICIES AND PROCEDURES

GENERAL CHURCH POLICIES

DISTRIBUTION OF FINANCES
Policy concerning distribution of money and food by deacons.

Any poor family requesting food for the first time will not be denied. The distribution will be made by request forms. Only nutritious food will be donated, no money, no sweets. There may be an appeal to the body for funds to purchase the groceries.

Any financial need will then be determined as valid. Vision is not a welfare ministry. Money, clothing and food will be given for the purposes of restoring its members into a right relationship with God. An advisor will be appointed to help this person budget and teach them about stewardship.

All appropriate local agencies may be contracted for help. In order for a needy member to understand God's laws of sowing and reaping, it is preferable for the person receiving funds to work at the church in return for the assistance given.

FIVE PRIMARY MINISTRY GOALS

Evangelism leads to individual disciple building, which leads to Christlike sonship, which leads to church building, which brings glory to God as the end of all efforts. Leadership should be always improving, not remaining stagnate.

JOB DESCRIPTIONS are to give a framework of expectation and are not meant to be dogmatic. However, leadership advancement is dependent upon meeting prescribed expectations. These descriptions are given according to Ex. 18:19-21, in order to accomplish goals. These may be modified and changed to better fit current situations.

LEADERSHIP MEETINGS are tentatively scheduled for the 3rd Saturday of each month at 9:30 a.m. They are to keep everyone updated and current with the business and progress of the church activities. Everyone is welcome; all leaders are expected to attend. The function of this meeting is overview, specific problems will be handled at another time, (please schedule). Prayer and encouragement are offered for any department needing it.

LEADERS

1. A leader is one walking in a life of repentance and communion with God. This person must be willing to attend scheduled meetings (if possible), i.e., leadership or group sessions.
2. Must be willing to screen all classes being taught, making certain that all teaching lines up with the vision of this body.
3. If approved purchases are made and you desire reimbursement, please put itemized receipts in offering box. If you desire to donate and wish a donation recorded please give us the receipt so notated.
4. In order to honor one another, let us not use supplies unless you have obtained permission from the person for whom they were intended.
5. The church facilities are not playgrounds, but instruction centers, help us keep order in the House of the Lord.
6. All leaders are expected to have completed *New Beginnings* and *Journey to Wholeness*, and to have read *40 Days to the Promise* and *Building the Church God Wants*.
7. Budgets must be submitted each December in order for plans to be made for the following year.
8. Any copying must be done prior to pre-service prayer, not during.
9. Will try to attend pre-service prayer. (9:30 a.m. Sunday)
10. Monthly schedules must be completed and a copy given to the chairman, for review, at the beginning of each Leadership meeting.
11. Each department is encouraged to plan activities and fellowship for their helpers, and/or for the body. Please invite the Leaders to attend; they want to be a part of what you are doing.
12. Leaders must structure short-term goals in order for long-term goals to happen. We all must be trained so we can grow. We build for tomorrow with clear objectives and goals.

    a. To be God's representative to the church, be a model.

    b. To show others how to walk, knowing that Kingdom character is first developed by observation.

    c. To explain duties to be performed.

    d. To discipline the followers of Christ (make disciples).

13. Leaders are expected to regularly and faithfully attend scheduled services.

14. Leaders are teachable, willing to serve, prepared, and faithful.

15. Their monthly meeting will compile a Church Calendar for the following month.

BOARD OF DIRECTORS

The Board is the official, civil and legal arm of the church.

1. The voting Board of Directors shall be officers of the Corporation and shall have the power to designate the spending of money.

    a. The number of Directors shall be four to seven. They shall be residents of San Diego County and members in good standing with Vision.

    b. The financial and legal affairs of the church shall be managed by the Board according to the Bylaws and Articles of Incorporation.

    c. Directors shall keep the "books" of the church.

    d. Directors shall establish the reasonable compensation for services.

2. Advisors (Church council), to the Board may be selected for specific projects and purchases.

3. General reports and plans will be given at leadership meetings.

4. Board members may be included on leadership sessions when necessary.

5. Annual Budgets of each department will be subject to the Board.

6. The Board of Directors establishes and annually reviews locally licensed or ordained ministers.

7. The Treasurer reports to the annual Board meeting.

8. The Board reports expenditures to the leadership meeting following the annual Board meeting in February.

GIFTS OF THE SPIRIT

1. We allow much freedom in the administration of the gifts of the Spirit.
2. Order will be maintained.
3. Proper ministry will be acknowledged. Improper uses will be judged and corrected. The first misuse will be corrected privately if possible. Please be open to learn to flow with the body in this manner. Let us embrace correction.
4. Should a particular time seem inappropriate, the Minister in charge has the authority to ask you to hold until another time.
5. Ministry should flow together with a similar topic, mood, or idea. If what you have does not agree please do not give it. Quite possibly, if you wait, a better time will emerge later. We strive to excel in the gifts.
6. For the protection of all, we expect that personal prophecy (directive words to a single person) be given in public (to be judged), or by seasoned or approved Ministers.

OFFERINGS

1. Vision believes in a willing offering given without coercion or guilt. This is a founding principle of this body.
2. If you are asked to receive finances for a public offering, you must keep this guideline in line.

   a. It would be proper to read from the Scripture to make your point valid.
   b. A short victory report of a blessing is in order.
   c. You may pray before or after the offering. If it is taken publicly then it should be dedicated publicly.

3. The offering should never take over 5 minutes, letting people know the need, and the blessing of this sacrament.
4. A public offering is planned as a portion of the worship service, to be taken each meeting.
5. Giving to God is a principle of paramount importance. We have no support other than from this local body. We thank you for your confidence in this ministry.

6. It is in giving that we receive. Vision Christian Church International tithes to other ministries.
7. Tithing, alms giving and donations are the duty of the believer. Accomplishing the vision of this body is dependent upon the member's faithfulness in this area.
8. We can only record your giving if you put your name on the tithe envelope or write a check. Anonymous giving cannot be deducted from your taxes.
9. A tax receipt is given at the end of the year from the Treasurer.

SPECIAL PROJECTS – (act with approval)

To be available to handle special projects, when they are mutually agreeable.

Standard: agreement to fulfill a special project is not unreasonably withheld.

WORKING RELATIONSHIPS

1. Report to the Senior Minister or the Assistant Pastor, and under their direct authority.
2. Obtain reports from and give cooperative direction to the leaders of the various groups in the music and arts ministry.
3. Work closely with the audio booth personnel in achieving the best possible musical sound, but with final authority belonging to the sound engineer.
4. Work closely with the office manager in arranging the calendar of events, but with final scheduling authority belonging to the office manager.

CLOSING THE SERVICE

If you are called to close a service, it should be done as follows:

1. A prayer pertinent to the message.
2. Or a prayer with a blessing and a way of getting people involved with each other.
3. You are not to re-preach the message or have your own service.
4. You may call for a salvation response if it has not already been done and if it is appropriate.

EVANGELISM

Principal function is to assist the Evangelist in the ministry of evangelism, missions, crusades and other outreaches.

1. Read and study the Word on evangelism.
2. Make local tracts.
3. Determine costs and get financial assistance.
4. Make necessary contacts for resources and help. Learn how to get help.
5. Maintain exemplary relations with all persons being worked with, portray Godly characteristics, be an example to others.
6. Attend regular meetings.
7. Have a vision for this project. Make a plan.
8. Build skills of evangelism in others, recruit.
9. Initiate actions to assist victims of calamities as an outreach to the community.
10. Learn to share and impart the Word of God to all people.
11. Learn to love mankind, get a heart for the lost.
12. Be open to the Holy Spirit for new ideas and projects. His ideas will work, while ours will just distract us from the center of His will.
13. Disciple the new convert until he/she can stand alone. Teach them to win souls.

NEWSLETTER AND BULLETIN PERSONNEL

Accountable to Office Secretary

1. Ideas, church goals, poems, testimonials, want ads, jokes, projects, outings, scriptures, editorials, featured families, fund raising drives, puzzles, and trivia, would be suitable material for articles.
2. All work must be completed neatly, readably and professionally. It is assumed that the grammar and punctuation will be properly edited. Our standards must be high.
3. Is it clear? concise? forceful and organized? informative?
4. All articles are subject to editing, revisions.
5. Hopefully, most announcements can go in the weekly bulletin.

BULLETIN BOARDS

1. Should be changed monthly.

2. One decorated board in the sanctuary should have designated space for letters, newspaper articles and personal data.
3. All used material on boards should be filed and kept at the church for future use if possible.
4. Should try to be in harmony with themes presented in the service.

STREET SIGN

1. All slogans will be pertinent, catchy, and accurate.
2. All slogans will have the approval of the church leadership.
3. All slogans will be presented in one month segments to the leadership meeting.
4. The sign-board will be changed weekly.
5. The words will be centered, with proper visual impact being a major concern.
6. The sign person may have contests for new slogans, and may purchase necessary books for ideas.
7. This job demands much prayer and creativity.

ANNOUNCEMENTS

1. First time visitors are to be acknowledged after the opening song, before the Word. They are to receive LOUD acknowledgement from the congregation and given free gifts and/or tokens of welcome.
2. If at this time members have been away for a time, their presence may be recognized.
3. Announcements for upcoming events should be in bulletin and then an additional mention may be made from pulpit only if necessary.
4. All announcements must be cleared prior to the service.

TESTIMONIES

1. Testimonies should be about the goodness of God.
2. They should be short, interesting, zippy, and encouraging.
3. This is not the time to preach, or to complain.
4. We want to hear what God has done in your life, be personal.

VISION CHRISTIAN CHURCH INTERNATIONAL
MISSIONS DEPARTMENT
THE PURPOSE

This department has been established to develop and encourage communication with the present Missionary families that we as a church support financially and spiritually. We desire to supply those families with current activities here at the church as well as gaining information as to what is "happening on the mission field." The goal is to communicate on a monthly basis to every family that we are supporting.

I. MONTHLY CORRESPONDENCE

A. Letters of encouragement to be sent to each missionary family we support at least once a month.

1. Letter is to go out the week following "Missions Sunday"
2. It is to include:

   a. Monthly support check.
   b. An update of what is currently happening at Vision since the last communication with them. Give such details as Bible School information, size of congregation, areas that we are standing in agreement for, miracles that have taken place, numbers of people that have been saved, baptized in the Holy Spirit, special prayer requests, or anything that you think will be of interest to them.
   c. Give comments to those things that they write to us. Encourage them in the work that they are doing.
   d. Inspire communication from them as to what is happening on the Mission field. Example: new contacts that they have made, new areas that they have been able to penetrate, etc.

3. Lives of certain people that have been changed by their ministry. Get testimonies of individuals, pictures would be good too.
4. Encourage a photo exchange of pictures of Vision and pictures of their ministry in action.
5. Ask questions as to their children. Be sure to include them in your letters. Children, especially on the mission field, love to be mentioned and something personal said to them. Perhaps you

could include a little something "just for them." If the child is small then a message on a balloon is nice, if a child is older then perhaps some magazine articles of interest to them would be nice. BE CREATIVE!

B. Keep a record of all Birthdays of everyone in the mission field.

1. Send them a card in plenty of time for them to receive it.
2. Let them know that Vision wishes them a "Happy Birthday."
3. Purchase the cards ahead of time and have the Pastor sign all of the cards ahead of time as well as signing them from the church.

C. Find out what their needs are:

1. Spiritually
2. Socially (are they lonely or in need in this area?)
3. Naturally (are there any needs for clothing, food, etc.)

II. KEEP AN ACCURATE FILING SYSTEM on each missionary family.

File separately:

A. A list of names of entire family, current address on the field, and their contact address in the United States. Phone numbers and e-mail addresses, if possible.
B. List the names with the birth dates.
C. List on a paper, the date that you wrote to them, the amount of the money that was sent to them, with the check number, and any response that was received.

(This way we can see "at a glance" all communication that has been made with each family.)

EXAMPLE: (subject to change)
date letter
amount of $ sent
check #
pictures sent?
birthday cards sent
date letter received
pictures received

D. Copy every letter that is sent to them and keep it in the file.

E. Keep every letter that is received from them in the appropriate file.

III. Mailing teaching cassettes

A. Each missionary family should have 10 teaching tapes sent to them each month. This will help keep them abreast of what is currently being taught at Vision.

B. Keep an accurate record in their file of the dates and the titles of the tapes sent to them and who did the work.

MISSIONS GOALS

"Go ye therefore, and teach all nations, baptizing them in the name of the Father, and of the Son, and of the Holy Ghost: Teaching them to observe all things whatsoever I have commanded you: and, lo, I am with you always, even unto the end of the world." (Matthew 28:19, 20)

1. To sponsor two primary short-term missions from the local church to Third-World countries.
2. To hold an Annual Missions Conference.
3. To assist in Mission awareness.
4. To assist Vision Christian Fellowship with World Evangelism Ministry.

MUSIC/WORSHIP GOALS

"Praise ye the Lord. Sing unto the Lord a new song, and his praise in the congregation of the saints...Let them praise his name in the dance: let them sing praises unto him with the timbrel and harp." (Ps. 149:1, 3)

1. Support evangelistic goals of overall church.
2. Train five (5) singers and identify and select five (5) musicians of different instruments to become part of the worship team.
3. Identify, train and utilize three (3) worship leaders.
4. Conduct quarterly worship training seminars.
5. Develop backup music with words for music Home Group usage.

VISION CHRISTIAN CHURCH INTERNATIONAL
MUSIC MINISTRY APPLICATION

1. Name_____
2. Street_____ City_____ Zip_____
3. Home Phone _____Business phone_____
4. When were you born again?_____
5. When did you receive the baptism of the Holy Spirit with the evidence of speaking in tongues?_____
6. How long have you lived in the San Diego county area?
   _____
7. Do you consider Vision Christian Church International your church home? Yes_____ No_____
8. Are you a tithing member? Yes_____ No_____
9. Have you served in a music ministry before?
   Yes_____ No_____
10. Why are you no longer involved in that ministry?_____
11. Do you feel a definite call to the ministry of music?
    Yes _____No_____
12. Have you attended the membership classes?
    Yes_____ No_____
13. Do you play any musical instruments? _____If so, please list them_____
14. What musical training do you have?_____
15. Do you smoke? _____
    Do you drink alcoholic beverages?_____
16. How long have you been coming to Vision?_____
17. Have you ministered in a church before?_____
    Where?_____
18. Are you willing to go through special training in this particular area of ministry?_____
19. Are you willing to pray daily for this ministry?_____
20. Do you agree to be at Friday evening and Sunday morning services, whether or not you are ministering?
    Yes _____No_____

As a music minister at Vision Christian Church International, you are required to:

1. Be prompt: we will expect you 45 minutes before the service starts.
2. To minister for other occasional special services and seminars.
3. To attend rehearsals regularly, which are held every Thursday evening at 7:00 p.m. unless otherwise noted.
4. To attend service regularly, even though you may not be ministering in that particular service.
5. To take direction from those in authority.
6. Adhere to the codes of conduct and dress of this position.

UNDERSTAND AND AGREE TO THESE CONDITIONS. PLEASE SIGN BELOW.

_____

SIGNATURE OF APPLICANT

_____

DATE

VISION CHRISTIAN FELLOWSHIP
MUSIC MINISTRY QUESTIONNAIRE
Name_____
Address_____
City _____State _____Zip_____
Phone (_____)_____
Work (_____)_____Ext.(_____)
Best time to call_____
Distance (minutes by car) from V.C.C.I._____
How long have you attended V.C.C.I.?_____

Instrument	Years playing	Read Music?
1.		
2.		
3.		
4.		
5.		

Principal Instrument_____
Do you sing well?_____
Why do you want to minister musically at V.C.C.I.?_____

Have you ever taken music lessons? _____ Where?_____
Have you ever taken voice lessons? _____ Where?_____
What part of the music ministry are you interested in?_____
What are your personal goals?
       Present_____

       Future_____
Do you have any suggestions that would help improve the music ministry
here?_____
How will you prepare spiritually to minister a V.C.C.I.?_____

_____
_____
_____

VISION FOR HOME FELLOWSHIPS

At the direction of the Holy Spirit, we are moving into a new realm in meeting the needs of our Body here at Vision Christian Church International and of our community through Home Fellowships. Our number one emphasis will be that of Outreach and Evangelism. Secondly, our emphasis will be on Pastoral Care through the groups. All of the saints are to be prepared to minister in winning others to Christ, training, equipping, and caring for them and again in turn, sending them out to do the work of the ministry. (Luke 4:18, Mark 16:15-18, Ephesians 4:11-12.)

The Home Fellowships will cover the five basic areas of the ministry which are clearly stated in the Vision of Vision. They are:

1. Worship and Praise - Approximately 10 to 15 minutes should be spent in magnifying the Lord and exalting the name of Jesus, through singing, praising and worshipping.
2. Prayer - A time should be spent praying for specific requests, for needs, and for others outside of your own group. Special emphasis should be made on praying for the government, for the Pastor and staff, for the schools, and for the missionaries that we are associated with as a church.
3. Teaching the Word of God - There will be special teachings prepared each week, in order to provide for uniformity of teaching throughout all of the Home Fellowships. (Each leader will teach

the outline and then be free to add illustrations, etc. that will enhance the teaching for their respective group.)

4. Fellowship - There should be approximately 10 to 15 minutes devoted to sharing, in which each person will have an equal time to share what is on his own heart.

5. Evangelism - The Home Fellowships are to be places of evangelism and outreach. We are to make a purposeful effort to reach out to the unchurched and unsaved, to communicate God's truths to them, to love them, to answer their questions, and to meet their needs. (The gifts of the Spirit will be in operation as the Home Fellowship's leaders and assistants in each group minister to the people, thus edifying and strengthening them.)

The key to success of the Home Fellowships will be you, the leader, and prayer. Any failure in the group will be a failure in prayer. You should be committed to a minimum of one hour a day in intercession for your group and for the individual people in your group.

We know that another key to success is your personal involvement in the vision of these meetings. You must be committed to the local church and the vision that God has given in this area. You will also want to see that you get to know other people in the church, and invite them to your home. You will also want to be sure who you get together with the assistant minister that will be working with you to pray together for these meetings. There is power in agreement. (Matthew 18:19)

We see that these groups are a strength to the local church as well as an outreach to the community.

SCRIPTURAL BASIS FOR HOME FELLOWSHIP GROUPS

A. Old Testament - Exodus 18:13-27, Numbers 11:16-17

1. Pastor's responsibility to see the flock taken care of:

    a. Be for the people Godward (intercession)
    b. Teach them ordinance and laws, corporately.
    c. Show them work they are to do.
    d. Get able men.

B. New Testament

1. Acts 1:12-14 - Upper room - Pentecost.
2. Acts 2:46 - Meet house to house
3. Acts 5:41-42 - Peter and apostles teaching in homes.
4. Acts 8:3 - Saul entered houses to destroy church.
5. Acts 10:22-24 - Peter shares Christ with Cornelius in home.
6. Acts 12:12 - Believers praying for Peter in a house.
7. Acts 18:5-8 - Justus' house.
8. Acts 20:20 - Paul taught house to house.
9. Acts 28:30-31 - Paul preaches in his own house.
10. Romans 16:3-5 - and I Corinthians 16:19 - Church in home of Aquila and Priscilla.
11. Colossians 4:15 - Church in home of Nymphas.
12. Philemon 1:2 - Church in his home.

INTERCESSION FOR HOME FELLOWSHIP - ZECHARIAH 4:6

A. Spiritual Warfare Weapons

1. Armor of God - Eph. 6:11-18.
2. Word of God - Eph. 6:11-18.
3. Name of Jesus - Phil. 2:9-11, Mark 16:17.

B. Our Authority as Believers

1. Jesus triumphed over Satan - Colossians 2:15
2. Bind and loosing - Mt. 18:18; Mt. 12:29; Mt. 10:8.

C. Groups That Intercede for Home Fellowships

1. Leaders, assistants and group intercessor.
   Meet before meeting or another day of the week.
2. Pastor, staff and Home Fellowship leaders, weekly at training session.
3. Church intercessors - Monday thru Friday at 5:30 a.m.
4. Pastoral and Executive staff - weekly.

SCRIPTURAL REQUIREMENTS FOR HOME FELLOWSHIP
LEADERS

I. Godly Characteristics for Men - I Tim. 3:1-7; Titus 1:5-9
   A. Above reproach.
   B. Husband of one wife.
   C. Temperate.
   D. Prudent.
   E. Respectable.
   F. Hospitable.
   G. Able to teach.
   H. Not given to wine.
   I. Not self willed.
   J. Not quick tempered.
   K. Not pugnacious.
   L. Uncontentious.
   M. Gentle.
   N. Free from love of money.
   O. One who manages his own household well.
   P. A good reputation with those outside the church.
   Q. Love what is good.
   R. Just.
   S. Devout.
   T. Not a recent convert.

II. Godly Characteristics for Women - Titus 2:3-5; I Peter 3:1-4
   A. Worthy of respect.
   B. Not a malicious talker.
   C. Temperate.
   D. Trustworthy in everything.
   E. Reverent.
   F. Not slanderous.
   G. Not addicted to much wine.
   H. Teach what is good.
   I. Love their husband and children.
   J. Self-controlled.
   K. Pure.
   L. Busy at home.
   M. Kind.
   N. Subject to their husbands.

III. Both Men and Women.

   A. Faithfulness - Luke 16:10
   B. Commitment - Luke 14:28-33
   C. Love people - John 15:12
   D. Desire to minister - II Cor. 5:18

DUTIES AND REQUIREMENTS OF WEEKLY HOME FELLOWSHIP LEADERS

1. To understand and be in agreement with the vision of the Pastor and be dedicated to carrying out that vision.
2. To care for and minister to the people who attend your group.
3. To keep records of weekly attendance and special ministry and turn them in promptly to your district leader.
4. To follow-up on all absentees from your group and call all group members weekly to love and encourage them.
5. Your assistants will pattern themselves after you, the leader, so be careful to stay within the guidelines of this ministry.
6. Be willing to commit approximately 10 hours per week to the success of your group.

   a. Weekly training session - 2 hours.
   b. Your group - 2 hours.
   c. Study and Intercession for your group - 3 hours.
   d. Follow-up calls and visits - 3 hours.

7. Be able to attend weekly training sessions.
8. Be in at least one service a week at Vision.
9. Attend monthly district meeting with the District Leader.

DUTIES AND REQUIREMENTS OF WEEKLY HOME FELLOWSHIP ASSISTANT

1. Have completed or be in the process of completing the Foundation classes at Vision.
2. To seek to understand and be in agreement with the vision of the Pastor and be dedicated to carrying out that vision.
3. To be in a submissive role to the Leader.
4. To be willing to take over different parts of the meeting as the leader asks and be able to teach a Home Fellowship.

5. Be willing to start a new group when the present group grows to about 15 steady attendees.
6. Be faithful in attendance at the group meeting and pray for the leaders.
7. Be willing to help promote group growth (remember, as you sow seeds as an assistant, you will be able to reap the fruit of them as you become a leader.)

GUIDELINES FOR HOME FELLOWSHIP GROUPS

1. The assigned lesson must be taught. The only ones allowed to teach the lesson are the Home Fellowship Leader, Assistant or those in training.
2. The goal of the groups is three-fold: evangelism, pastoral care, and equipping the saints.
3. Start the meeting on time, regardless of how many there are. God will bless this.
4. Keep accurate written reports on group attendance and special ministry (praise reports that occur in the group). Turn these monthly reports in to your district leader.
5. Leaders have a choice of having their meetings on Monday, Thursday, Friday or Saturday evening, or having a day meeting on any day except Sunday. They must meet once a week.
6. The time frame of each meeting is 1 1/2 hours.
7. At the end of the designated time for the meeting, those desiring to leave should be given the opportunity to do so. If others want to stay for fellowship and ministry, they may.
8. Follow the structural plan given by Pastor. All 5 basic areas of ministry are to be part of every meeting. This is required.
9. Food is to be served before or after the meeting. Beverages (coffee or tea) may be served during the meeting, if the leader so desires. Use this time for fellowship.
10. An offering is to be received at each meeting along with a short teaching or testimony on "Giving." Let the people know the offering goes to the Church and that they can designate their giving.
11. Don't let people you don't know minister to your group. The gifts are to flow under your guidance and leadership. Protect the sheep.
12. Leaders must pick up all follow-up cards weekly from their assigned boxes.

13. Leaders must distribute visitor packets to each newcomer. The Home Fellowship leader is responsible for all material given out (salvation, Baptism of Holy Spirit, Healing tracts, and visitor packets.
14. Make phone calls to anyone absent from the meeting.

DELEGATION IN HOME FELLOWSHIP GROUPS

A. Delegation is God's will

1. Numbers 11:10-17
2. Matthew 28:19-20
3. Acts 6:18

B. How to Delegate

1. Plan
2. Instruct
3. Organize
4. Monitor

C. Ministry of the Believer

1. The call to serve - John 15:16
2. Saints do the work of the ministry - Eph. 4:11-12
3. All believers are ministers of reconciliation - II Cor. 5:18
4. Believers are able ministers - II Cor. 3:56
5. Works prepared - Eph. 2:10
6. Equipped to minister

   a. Gifts of the Holy Spirit - I Cor. 12:8-11
   Word of Wisdom, Word of Knowledge, Faith, Gifts of Healing, Working of Miracles, Prophecy, Discerning of Spirits, Tongues, Interpretation of Tongues.
   b. Motive Gifts - Rom. 12:6-8
   Prophecy, Serving, Teaching, Exhorting, Giving, Leadership, Mercy.

D. Areas to Delegate

1. Assistant
2. Praise and Worship leader
3. Children's Leader
4. Intercessor
5. Record Keeper
6. Counselor
7. Greeter
8. Follow-up Caller

   a. In Class: warning and separation of child from group in class. After two warnings and attempts to bring control, refer to supervisor.
   b. Supervisor: adult who will assist in counseling child from Scriptures, then sending back to class if cooperative. If not, can remain with supervisor or returned to parent (if available), depending on child's compliance and attitude.

At no time will corporal discipline be used by any staff at VCCI without written permission by the children's parents.

SCHEDULE: Attached you will find a schedule for teaching assignments for the next quarter. We will attempt to schedule teachers and assistants for a 3-month (quarter) period, for one service only. Teachers will be required to attend the other service (if scheduled) in the morning, or if not, the evening service and Wednesday Home Groups.

ABSENCES: Should a teacher be unable to perform his/her duties, it is their responsibility to find a replacement with the help of your Sunday Superintendent. He/she will ensure that material is dispersed for classroom instruction. Our first choice will be the assistant teacher.

TRAINING: Twice a quarter a teacher meeting will be held to determine needs, discuss problems, develop solutions, and train for more effective ministry. (To be announced).

LEADING BIBLE DISCUSSION

I. Three Basic rules for successful discussion

A. Wait your turn
  1. Let person finish talking before another starts
  2. If two start to speak at once - leader chooses who goes first; give other opportunity next.
  3. Conversation is directed toward whole group.
  4. Courtesy.

B. Stay on Topic.
C. Keep it brief.
D. Stress these rules each week until group is flowing well.

II. Possible Difficulties
  A. Unrelated Comments
    1. Don't ignore it.
    2. Don't allow silence.
    3. Don't say, "That's off the topic!"
    4. Don't put the person down.
    5. Establish relationships with each group member.
    6. Try to bring conversation back to topic.
    7. Try to relate what was said to topic.
    8. Build a bridge.
    9. Speak to person privately if this is a constant problem.
    10. Sometimes the Holy Spirit may want to change direction.

  B. Theological Problems
    1. Some issues have been debated for centuries.
    2. Can cause division and strife.
    3. How to proceed.
        a. Decide for yourself the value of discussing it.
        b. Proceed with wisdom - not emotion.
        c. Share your own insights.
        d. Do not allow group to get sidetracked.
    4. Difference of opinion.
        a. Can be profitable.
        b. Refer to Word.
        c. Walk in Love.

  C. Wrong Interpretations
    1. Occasionally someone will contribute something obviously incorrect.

a. Acknowledge contribution in positive manner.
b. Ask others to share viewpoint.
c. Don't say, "No, that is not right!"
d. Refer to Scriptures.
e. Don't try to force.
f. Walk in love.

D. The Person Who Tries to Dominate
   1. Speak to them privately.
   2. Appreciate their contributions.
   3. Remind them of 3 basic rules.
   4. Enlist support in helping draw out others.
   5. Direct questions to others.

TECHNIQUES IN ASKING QUESTIONS

1. Are the questions brief and clear?
2. Do the questions stimulate discussion?
3. Are your questions relevant to the purpose of the discussion?
5. Use first names as you talk. This is a discipline that has its rewards. People want their contributions personalized and the first name adds that personal and loving touch.
6. Answer questions with questions. This keeps the discussion leader from answering all the questions and in many cases the person is asking a question because of a hidden desire to tell what he or she thinks. Sometimes the leader may say, "What do you think?" You may want to also throw the question open to others by saying, "How would the rest of you answer this question?" By answering questions, the group works harder at the discovery process. Do not deprive the group members of the excitement of personal discovery. Someone has said, "People enjoy climbing mountains, but only the feeble enjoy being carried up."
7. Value an individual's response in your group. The leader may not share the viewpoint, but he can affirm each person along with his or her thoughts and ideas.
8. Don't embarrass a person by asking a question that has the potential of frightening the individual.
9. Give one the opportunity of "passing." Forced sharing at an introductory level can be very harmful.

10. Avoid advice giving. A time of sharing can be stifled by giving advice, by not listening, and by judging.
11. Discourage vague sharing that deals with impersonal generalities.
12. Begin early sessions with sharing questions from the past. Work up to the present and then into the future.
13. If possible connect the sharing question with the content of the study.

COUNSELING PRINCIPLES

1. Always remember counselee's name. Address person by first name, unless otherwise indicated by counselee.
2. Be a good listener, watch your expression and don't act shocked by what you hear.
3. Make sure you have fresh breath and a pleasant fragrance.
4. Pray without ceasing, giving thanks and praise in all circumstances. Pray before you counsel.
5. It's God's ability in you, so trust Him to guide and direct you as you counsel. You are led by the Spirit of God.
6. The words you speak will be remembered long after you have forgotten them, so be as wise as a serpent but gentle as a dove.
7. Always walk in love, as faith works by love. The counselee is hoping you will have answers to his problems, and we know God has answers to all problems.
8. Be a doer of the Word. Use the Name of Jesus and speak directly to the problem. Do not say what you are going to do, but do the Word.
9. Show counselee he is not wrestling with flesh and blood, but principalities and spiritual powers. Share how to intercede and tear down strongholds by prayer and speaking the Word.
10. Your word is your bond. If you make a promise, keep it. Don't get caught up in the emotion of the situation and say you'll do something you don't want to do. Don't let those you counsel know your personal life or they may snare you.
11. Encourage counselee not to be moved by adverse circumstances, as these things are temporal and subject to change. The Word changes you and the situation. Trust in God, regardless of the circumstances.
12. Familiarize yourself with principles of agreement, praise, favor,

intercession. Be led by the spirit and share victory experiences only. Be led by the Spirit, not open doors.

14. Always expect to have signs following as you operate in the Spirit. Be wise when you speak, for God will use who He wills. Desire genuineness of the Spirit.
15. Seek counsel of the godly, someone you can trust.
16. Remember, you are to do all things as unto the Lord and you'll be blessed. To whom much is given much is required.
17. You can do all things through Christ who strengthens you. Wean people off of you.
18. Don't condemn, criticize, preach, talk down to or get loud. Watch your tone of voice, and speak in love.
19. Counselee has to make all the decisions. We can only suggest, not dictate.
20. Never counsel someone to stop taking medicine, get a divorce, or do anything contrary to Scriptures.
21. Don't allow counselee to dwell on the problem. Give him homework in the Scriptures. If he doesn't get in the Word and keeps on with problems, ask yourself, "Should I keep counseling this person?" Often people make confessions out of fear.
22. Don't touch the person any more than necessary.
23. Don't counsel a person of the opposite sex privately. If asked to go to someone's home, take someone with you.

VISION OF VISION

Jesus Christ is our foundation, our Lord, our growth, our fullness, and our life. In Him we have five main expressions to our lives. They are:

A LIFE OF WORSHIP...singing psalms, hymns, and spiritual songs; musical instruments; dancing unto the Lord.

A LIFE OF PRAYER...petitions, commands, intercession, prayer of faith, and the prayer of agreement.

A LIFE OF FELLOWSHIP...working, caring, sharing, and worshipping together.

A LIFE OF GOD'S WORD...teaching, preaching, and equipping the believer to do the work of the ministry.

A LIFE OF EVANGELISM...fulfilling the command to "GO YE" into the world, telling the "GOOD NEWS" of Jesus Christ.

All that you, as a believer will do in your life in Christ Jesus will be in one or more of these five areas. We ask that you prayerfully consider the vision of Vision Christian Church International, and each of its aspects as you read it.

We want you to be fulfilled in Him.

VISION CHRISTIAN CHURCH INTERNATIONAL
Sunday School

Policy and Procedures

PURPOSE: To train and teach the children involved with Vision Christian Fellowship in Biblical concepts designed to:

GOALS:
1. Lead them into a personal relationship with our Lord Jesus Christ
2. Strengthen them to become committed disciples of Christ.
3. Assist the parents of the children in Christian character development and discipline of their children.
4. Utilize the Sunday School Department as a training forum for ministry development.

PROCEDURES: Except when special services interfere, the Sunday School will function every Sunday morning, 52 weeks per year in conjunction with regular Worship services. For ages 0-11 it will consist of two components:
1. Corporate worship.
2. Sunday School training and teaching.

All children, except nursery age, will begin in the sanctuary for Praise and Worship. This is designed to allow the children to experience being a part of the larger community of believers. Upon the dismissal of the children from the worship center, they will proceed to their respective classes. The class will include:
1. 2-3 year olds.
2. 4-5 year olds.

3. 6-7 year olds.
4. 8-11 year olds.

They will meet in their classes for the approximate 45 minutes of class time to complete a pre-determined lesson planned by the teacher and supervised by the Sunday School Superintendent and Pastoral staff. The teachers for the 2-5 year olds will remain with their children until parents receive them. The 6-11 year olds can be released upon the completion of the regular service.

PERSONNEL:
Supervising Pastor:
Sunday School Superintendent:
Teachers:
Assistant Teachers:

DISCIPLINE: Should a child be disruptive in class, the following procedures are to be followed:
1. Verbal correction
2. Separation (time out)
3. Removal by calling parent

MINISTRY OF FOLLOW-UP GOALS
"I pray not that thou shouldest take them out of the world, but that thou shouldest keep them from evil. They are not of this world, even as I am not of this world." (John 17:15,16)
1. Develop and implement a system of follow-up for V.C.C.I. visitors and an outreach to New Christians.
2. Develop and implement a computerized database information system on each visitor, New Christian, and V.C.C.I. to support effective follow-up and communications.
3. Develop and implement a system of reporting and accountability for home fellowship leaders.
4. Develop reporting forms and follow-up flow chart.

MINISTRY OF HELPS GOALS
"Then the twelve called the multitude of the disciples unto them, and said, It is not reason that we should leave the word of God, and serve tables. Wherefore, brethren, look ye out among you seven men of honest report, full of the Holy Ghost and wisdom, whom we may appoint over this

business. But we will give ourselves continually to prayer, and to the ministry of the word." (Acts 6:2-4)

1. To train and commission Deacons, I Tim. 3:8-13 to oversee the functions of the Helps of Ministry. This will include:
   a. Ushers
   b. Hospitality Helpers
   c. Food & Clothing outreach for the poor.
   d. Building maintenance Coordinator

YOUTH DEPARTMENT GOALS

"And that from a child thou hast known the holy Scriptures, which are able to make thee wise unto salvation through faith which is in Christ Jesus." (II Tim. 3:15)

1. Meet weekly or more often as needed for ministry activity
2. Develop quarterly advances for youth program.
3. Increase youth group attendance by 50%.
4. Develop:
   a. Youth Pastor.
   b. Assistant Youth Pastor.
   c. Youth Leaders to help shepherd.
5. Train youth to disciple youth, using Christian Character Development material.
6. Get youth involved in Outreach and short term missions.

Of course, you may have many other policies and procedures for the running of a fellowship. These examples will help you understand the types of policies and procedures needed, and a method for documenting them for your congregation. Also, sample Policies and Procedures from our ministry, Vision International, are provided for you in Appendix 4.

Strategic Church Administration

"I would love to do the job you want me to do; if I only new what you want me to do I would do it."

- Frustrated Church Worker

Stan E. DeKoven, Ph.D.

CHAPTER 9

JOB DESCRIPTIONS

Job descriptions help everyone involved in ministry know what is expected from them as they labor in God's Kingdom. Many volunteer leaders, notwithstanding paid staff, have bitterly (and justifiably) complained that they rarely know what is expected, or feel overwhelmed or sabotaged in their service. A well written, clearly understood and agreed to position description helps insure the possibility of quality service, while minimizing confusion, needless duplication of effort, and subsequent frustration.

To follow are a cornucopia of position descriptions that can be used for your ministry.

PASTOR

Principal function: The pastor will shepherd the congregation, ministering and ruling in oversight over the congregation in spiritual and natural functions. The Pastor is to be in touch with God - himself and for the leading of the flock.

REGULAR DUTIES:

1. Regular pulpit ministry.
2. To counsel those seeking help who are unable to be served by the other appointed ministry.
3. To train leadership in the church with the help of other gift ministries (Eph 4:11-16).
4. Supervise the staff of the church.
5. Serve on the leadership of the church.
6. Oversee or initiate the oversight of Christian education of the believer.
7. Make those decisions which do not require the advice of functioning groups within the church.
8. Maintain relationships within and without the church with further building and maintaining of the Kingdom of God.
9. Host visiting ministries (or assign).

10. Evaluate church structure and functioning.
11. Supervise preparation of job descriptions and expectations.

Vision Statement

Our vision is to fulfill the Great Commission (Mt. 28), by effectively raising up a local New Testament Church, and thus evangelizing our world for Christ. Starting with the local Church, the developing and planting churches and Training Centers (in cooperation with Vision Christian College) will be our focus of ministry activity.

Goal: To develop an effective organizational flow for the purpose of the facilitation of the ministry vision. We, with God's help, intend to:

1. Win the Lost at any Cost;
2. Equip the saints for the work of the ministry;
3. Minister Healing to the Hurting;
4. Cover the Earth with God's Word

Objective: To describe, plan, and develop job statements and implement a ministry program to meet the vision and goals of the local church.

Introduction

You have been called to a role of leadership over an area vital to the reaching of the vision of Vision Christian Church International.

General Requirements

1. Attendance at Church each Sunday morning, Wednesday night Leadership Training, and faithfulness in the area of service the Lord has called you to. Should you be unable to fulfill your commitment for whatever reason (excepting an emergency, of course) you should take the initiative and responsibility to find a suitable replacement.
2. Commitment to minister to your position as unto the Lord.

All of the leadership of this God-ordained fellowship agree to the above vision, goals, objectives, and mutual covenant to one another, as the Lord gives us strength.

The Ministry Team	Co-Laborer for Christ

DOCTRINAL STATEMENT
OF
VISION CHRISTIAN CHURCH INTERNATIONAL

Article I

AIMS:

MISSION: The mission of this local church is best expressed by Paul in Romans 15:18-19, *"By word and deed, by the power of signs and wonders, by the power of the Holy Spirit, to preach the full gospel of Christ."*

IDENTITY: The character of this local church is best expressed in the following motto:

The Word of Christ preached
The Name of Christ believed
The Power of Christ experienced
The Love of Christ shared
The Coming of Christ expected

Note: The legal aspects of the church, as mandated by state law, are controlled by the Bylaws of the Corporation, Vision International College and University and managed by a Board of Directors, which meets from time to time. The daily life of the church is governed by this character, and by the pastors of the church, working with the Church Council. (See Article III, Sec. 2.1c)

ARTICLE II
DOCTRINE
SECTION I

General Statement

1. We generally accept those great doctrines of the Christian faith that have been adhered to from the beginning by all major branches of the Church.

2. We receive and proclaim the Bible as the only inspired and

authoritative revelation given to man by God, and we endeavor to conform all of our teaching and practice to its demands. All else that claims inspiration or authority must yield to the Bible.

3. Authority for determining the interpretation of Scripture is vested in the Board of Directors, except that nothing may be taught or practiced that is contrary to the Bylaws of the Corporation or this Charter.

SECTION 2

Particular Statement

SALVATION - We believe that for the individual, eternal life and inheritance of the kingdom of God depend upon:

1. Coming into spiritual union with Christ, which is achieved through:

   a. personal faith in the atoning value of His death
   b. confidence in the life-giving power of His resurrection
   c. declaring Him to be Savior and Lord (Rom. 10:9-11)

2. Yielding to the Lordship of Christ, through daily obedience to His will as revealed in Scripture and conscience.

Salvation is a product of faith, not of good works; but true faith will soon be demonstrated by righteous living.

HEALING - We believe that bodily healing is provided in the atonement, and that James 5:13-16 is a paradigm for the church today. This healing covenant does not preclude the use of medical science, but it does require all Christians to turn to the Lord in time of sickness, with an expectation that prayer and the laying-on of hands will facilitate their recovery.

CHURCH - We see two expressions of the Church.

1. The universal Church, which is "the body of Christ" on earth, built out of Christians from many denominations. Our local church is one small part of this greater world-wide church (Eph. 1:22-23).
2. The local church, which is the body of Christ within its own

community, called to be as Christ Himself would be if He were ministering in person in that place (Rom. 12:3-8). We do not disparage denominational groupings, but we think that the main emphasis in scripture is upon individual local churches, and we are striving to be such a church, operating in harmony with biblical principles as God has enabled us to understand them.

WORSHIP - We view the church as being primarily a worshipping community, and we believe that each local church can best fulfill its evangelistic mandate through the medium of powerful charismatic worship (I Cor. 14:24-25).

To that end, we place major emphasis upon creating a rich and mature worship style that will itself be an unmistakable witness of the presence of God, and that will fully equip the people to carry Christ into their everyday world.

We desire a worship-style that is joyful yet dignified, powerful yet reverent, one that combines the best of the old and of the new.

PENTECOST - We believe that every Christian should receive a personal baptism in the Holy Spirit, additional to the new birth, after the pattern described in the book of Acts and taught in the New Testament letters.

CHARISMATA - We believe that the diverse gifts of the Holy Spirit (the "charismata", I Cor. 12:8-11) should be freely operative in the church, and that it is the presence of these gifts that particularly equips the church to be as Christ himself would be if He were ministering in our locality.

FAITH - We rejoice in the restoration of biblical concepts of faith (Mark 11:22-24; Mt. 17:20-21; 21:20-22; John 15:7-8; 16:23-24; etc.). Vigorous faith is the key to answered prayer and to successful appropriation of the many promises of God. Without such faith it is impossible to please God (Heb. 11:6). By faith alone can the work of God properly be done (I John 5:4-5).

PROSPERITY - We believe it is God's ordinary intention that his people should enjoy prosperity and good health (III John 2; John 10:10). However, the promises of prosperity do have certain conditions attached to them: such as, "delight yourself in the Lord" (Ps. 37:3-6); "abide in Christ" (John 15:4-7); be faithful in "tithes and offerings" (Malachi 3:6-12, Luke 6:38), etc.

To this end, we teach people to be generous in their giving, to use the tithe as their standard, and in all things to trust God to meet their every need - spiritual and material.

LIFESTYLE - We affirm the world God has made, and we receive it with Thanksgiving, believing that God has "given us all things to enjoy" (I Tim. 6:17). We do not seek to impose a narrow conformism upon people, nor a restrictive legalism, but rather to help them to be all that God has made them to be, and to do all that God has given them to do.

In general, we condemn only what is clearly condemned in Scripture; otherwise, we allow people liberty to fulfill themselves in their own ways, subject to the principle of living concern for one's neighbor (Rom. 14:1-23).

TALENTS - Our aim is to create opportunities for every person to serve, whether teaching, administration, hospitality, nurture, counseling, music, song, dance, art, drama, sculpture, and so on (Rom. 12:3-8).

DISCIPLESHIP - All Christians are expected to be true disciples of the Lord Jesus Christ and to give to Him alone their absolute allegiance. Our aim therefore is to disciple people to Christ, and to bring them to obedience to His will.

Hence, we do not aspire to disciple people to a church, nor to a creed, nor to any man.

Nonetheless, as indicated below, it is rightly expected that the members of the church will ordinarily and gladly submit to the properly exercised oversight, ministry, and disciplines of the church.

However, we also recognize that each Christian, in the exercise of his or her spiritual priesthood, must retain a right to dissent from any authority save that of conscience (I John 2:27).

BAPTISM - Although we respect other views on the subject of baptism, we believe that the weight of Biblical evidence favors believer's baptism - that is, baptism by full immersion subsequent to a responsible and personal confession of faith in Christ.

We do not practice infant baptism, but we do encourage parents to bring their children to the Lord for a special act of dedication.

Thus, baptism is less than an agent of regeneration, but more than a mere memorial. A particular quality of the life of Christ is conveyed to those who go through its waters in obedient faith.

HOLY COMMUNION-Since communion is one of the few things that Christ specifically commanded his followers to do corporately, it seems incongruous to relegate it to an infrequent observance, or to treat it as a substantially unnecessary addendum to the regular church program.

For that reason, we may celebrate communion every Sunday morning as an integral part of our worship program.

We do not believe that a person's salvation depends upon taking communion each week, but we do teach that the communion is a powerful aid to dynamic Christian life, and that full maturity in Christ is hardly attainable without regular participation at the Lord's table.

For the person who eats and drinks with faith, Christ is present in the bread and the wine, and the communicant becomes a partaker of His divine grace. We do not attempt to define the nature of this presence of Christ in the communion elements, but we do affirm its reality (I Cor. 10:16; 11:29-30).

Hence our view of the communion is this:

-It is more than a mere memorial, for it is a channel of the grace of God;
-it is essential in order to remain Christian;
-yet it must be regularly kept as a vital part of each believer's growth in
 Christ.

PROCLAMATION - We have little confidence in organized programs for church growth, but every confidence in the power of the preached word to draw men and women to Christ (I Cor. 1:15-16; 10:8-17; I Cor. 9:16; II Tim. 4:2, etc.).

We are content to allow God to grow the church as big as he pleases; but we are not so much committed to building one large church as we are to sponsoring similar churches, thus creating many more opportunities for people to serve Christ. We believe that God's program for national renewal is to plant thousands of local churches, each powerful in the gospel.

PRAYER - We are committed to unremitting collective and individual prayer as the undergirding source of all real life and all worthwhile endeavor in the church. Perhaps the best places for such prayer, and for warm friendship, are home fellowship, in which we encourage each member of the church to participate.

ESCHATOLOGY - We believe that Christ will return to this earth at the end of the age, and that his return will result in the resurrection of the dead, the judgments of God, and the ultimate establishment of the eternal kingdom of God. We do not adhere to any particular system of prophetic interpretation, and we respect the diverse views that Christians have on these matters. We seek only the glory of God, by striving to present men and women to him perfect in Christ.

POLICIES OF THE CHURCH

The Senior Pastor

1. This church is set in order under the authority of the Bible and at the request of a company of believers in the Lord Jesus Christ, on the following principles: it is to be scripturally independent as to its faith and government (Heb. 6:12; Eph. 4:11-12; I Cor. 12:18-20); and in accord with the twelfth, thirteenth and fourteenth chapters of I Cor. as to its conduct and practice; and in cooperative fellowship with other bodies of believers who are "earnestly contending for the faith that was once delivered unto the saints" (Jude 3).
2. The government of the church is in the hands of the senior pastor, who has ultimate authority under Christ. He acts as chairman of all meetings of the church, except that he has the right to delegate that function to other persons.
3. No person may be invited to speak, preach, perform or otherwise minister in the church without the consent of the Senior Pastor.
4. In general, the Senior Pastor is expected to exercise his authority in conjunction with other senior ministers and/or officers of the church, and with the consent of the congregation. Neither the Pastors nor the congregation have absolute authority within the

church, but each should be willing at times to submit to the other, and all must submit to Christ - for authority in the church is neither autocratic, nor oligarchic, nor democratic, but theocratic. The church has only one prevailing task: to find the will of God, and to do it.

SECTION 2
Church Government
The Church Council

Following from the above -
1. We recognize four kinds of authority in the church.
   a. The absolute authority of Christ. Christ alone can be and must be the Chief Shepherd of the flock of God.
   b. The delegated authority of the under-shepherd. Christ chooses to express his authority through men and women who are His gift to the church (see Phil. 1:1; Heb. 13:17; Mt. 18:18; Acts 20:28; I Cor. 16:16; Eph. 4:11-12; I Thess. 5:12-13; etc.)

   The people are expected to yield to the authority of their bishop/minister/elder/presbyter/overseer (those terms are nearly synonymous in the New Testament).

   In this church we choose to call the person who occupies the office of the bishop or chief overseer, the "Senior Pastor." The authority given to the Senior Pastor in Scripture is forceful, and in all matters relevant to the spiritual life of the church, to its mission and growth, its discipline and order, his rule (when it is properly exercised) should be obeyed.

   c. The advisory authority of the presbytery. Since authority vested in one man alone may easily become tyranny (I Peter 5:3), and since Scripture commends the wisdom found in many counselors (Prov. 11:14; 24:6), and since there are diverse gifts and ministries in the body of Christ (I Cor. 12:14-27), the Senior Pastor is expected to work with a team of dedicated people (who may be called presbyters, elders, deacons, counselors, or the like).

   The New Testament clearly indicates that the full oversight of a local church should be vested in such a plural eldership, or ministry team

(Phil. 1:1; Acts 20:28; Titus 1:5). This collective leadership (headed by the Senior Pastor) creates a source of immense spiritual power (Mt. 18:18-20).

In this church, the above principles will be implemented by the setting up of a Church Council, which will consist of the Senior Pastor, all the assistant pastors, and an appointed group of lay men and women. The number of lay people on the council, the manner of their appointment, and the term of their office, are determined from time to time by the council itself.

This Church Council will meet approximately once each month, or at such times as it may determine, and it is responsible for the proper conduct of the affairs of the church, except that final authority shall remain vested in the Board of Directors of the Corporation in accordance with the Bylaws of the Corporation.

d. The priestly authority of the people. The pastor(s) and councilors must recognize the priesthood of each believer (I Peter 2:9; Rev. 1:6; 5:10; 20:6; Heb. 10:19-23; Rom. 5:1-5; Heb. 4:16; etc.). This priesthood means that the people need no intermediary save Christ to represent them before God. Hence, God may speak to the church at any time through the humblest saint - He is not bound to speak only to or through "official" channels. Hence, each member must be allowed a voice, and godly leaders will always be attentive to the voice of the people, and willing to obey at once if God's word should come to the church from that source.

Yet, final decisions must remain with the oversight, and ultimately with the Senior Pastor, who is responsible under God for the welfare of the church.

2. The Church must function as a theocracy.

In any growing congregation there will be people at all stages of spiritual growth and maturity. For that reason, it is usually not proper to submit the affairs of the church to a democratic vote, for the purpose of the church is not to do the will of the majority, but the will of God.

However, there will no doubt be issues from time to time in which the oversight might deem it advisable to learn the will of the people, and in which a democratic vote might be the best way to discover the will of God; therefore...

3. The members must be given a voice.

At least once a year, and more often if deemed necessary, a meeting of the church members will be called.

The purpose of this meeting is twofold: to allow reports to the church to be presented; and to allow the members of the congregation an opportunity to express their own opinions and ideas concerning the church.

The leaders of the church are required to give freedom to the people to express themselves in love, and to offer any constructive criticism or helpful comment.

The leaders are required to listen to the people with respect, and to be sensitive to the possibility that the Holy Spirit may be speaking to the church through any one of them.

Notice of the annual meeting of the church members shall be announced at least two weeks in advance, both from the pulpit and in the church bulletin.

ARTICLE IV

CHURCH MEETINGS

1. As nearly as possible, all church meetings shall be opened and closed with prayer.
2. The church shall assemble each Sunday for public worship and during the week as may be designated by the pastors. Nothing contained herein shall forbid suspension of one or more services when circumstances make such a suspension necessary.
3. The communion shall be celebrated as often as possible. All church members are expected to attend the communion service unless they are reasonably prevented from doing so (such as by illness, annual vacation, employment schedule, and the like).

ARTICLE V
CHURCH MEMBERSHIP

SECTION 1
Conditions for Membership
The church membership is comprised of those persons who:

- have accepted Jesus Christ as their personal Lord and Savior.
- agree to submit to the leadership of the church in matters of doctrine and Christian conduct, and in the disciplinary authority of the church.
- have been baptized in water subsequent to their confession of faith in Christ.
- have made written application to join the church, including a covenant not to pursue legal action to sue the Pastors, Directors, Trustees, or any other member of the church staff in connection with the performance of their official scriptural duties.
- agree to honor I Cor. 6:1-8.
- do not hold membership in any other church.
- agree to be faithful and generous in supporting the church financially.
- accept the rules and principles embodied in the Bylaws of the Corporation and in this Charter.

SECTION 2
New Members

1. New church members shall be brought into membership by the laying on of hands of the Pastors in a previously announced open meeting of the church.
2. Only those church members who are 12 years of age or older shall be entitled to speak on any matter put before the church members by the Board of Directors.
3. Applicants for church membership shall acknowledge publicly their commitment to the beliefs and practices of this church, and shall voluntarily and publicly confess their submission to the Pastors and other recognized leaders in matters pertaining to doctrine and Christian conduct.
4. The pastors, together with the recognized leadership of the church, shall

pledge themselves to shepherd, counsel and instruct the members in the ways of God.

5. Existing church members shall acknowledge their acceptance of the candidate(s) for church membership and shall commit themselves to love, nourish, and care for the new members.

SECTION 3
Arbitration Procedure:

Since the scriptures require Christians to take their disputes to the church and not to the civil courts (I Cor. 6:1-8), all disputes which may arise between any member of this church and any other members and the church itself (including any officer or director thereof), shall be resolved by binding arbitration if efforts to mediate or conciliate the dispute have failed. Either party to the dispute may initiate the arbitration process by filing with the other party a written request for arbitration within a reasonable time after the dispute has arisen and efforts to mediate or conciliate have failed. In such a case, both parties shall each name an arbitrator, and two so selected shall name a third. All arbitrators must be born-again Christians who have received the baptism of the Holy Spirit (according to Acts 2:4), and who are members in good standing of a local church as near as possible in kind to this church. The third arbitrator chosen by the other two shall disclose, before accepting the appointment, any financial or personal interest in the outcome of the appointment, any financial or personal interest in the outcome of the arbitration, and any existing or past financial, professional, family or social relationships, which are likely to affect impartiality or which might reasonably create an appearance of impartiality or bias. Either of the parties to the arbitration, on the basis of such disclosures, may disqualify such a candidate from continuing duty to disclose relationships or interests which may impair his impartiality. Either party, regardless of the stage of the arbitration process, may on the basis of such disclosures disqualify such a person from further participation. The arbitration process shall not proceed until the third arbitrator is selected.

The arbitration proceeding shall be conducted in accordance with the principles found in the Bible, with particular reference to I Cor. 6:1-8 and Mt. 18:15-20. The arbitrators shall appoint the time and place for the hearing and cause notification to the parties to be served personally or by registered mail not less than twenty days before the hearing.

Appearance at the hearing waives such notice. The arbitrators may adjourn the hearing from time to time as necessary and, on request of a party and for good cause, or upon their own motion, may postpone the hearing to a later date. The arbitrators may hear and determine the controversy upon the evidence produced notwithstanding the failure of a party duly notified to appear. The parties are entitled to be heard, to present evidence material to the controversy and to cross-examine witnesses appearing at the hearing. The hearing shall be conducted by all the arbitrators, but a majority of them may determine any question and render a final award. If, during the course of the hearing, an arbitrator for any reason ceases to act, he shall be replaced in the same manner in which he was originally selected. The arbitrators may, in their absolute discretion, admit as evidence any affidavit or declaration concerning the matters in dispute, a copy thereof having been given at least twenty days previously to the party against whom the same is offered, but the person whose evidence is so taken shall be subject to cross-examination by such party. The arbitrators shall have the power to order and direct what they shall deem necessary to be done by either submission of a dispute or arbitration shall not be revoked by the death of any party to the dispute, and any award will be binding upon such person's heirs and successors.

The decision of the arbitrators shall be binding on both parties, and both parties submit themselves to the personal jurisdiction of the courts of California, both state and federal, for the entry of a judgment confirming the arbitrator's award.

The arbitration process is not a substitute for any disciplinary process set forth in the Constitution or Bylaws of the church, and shall in no way affect the authority of the church to investigate reports of misconduct, conduct hearings, or administer discipline.

ARTICLE VI
CHURCH DISCIPLINE

SECTION I
The Biblical Pattern

Scripturally exercised discipline is one of the marks of a true church (Mt. 18:15-20; Rom. 16:17-18; I Cor. 5:1-13; Gal. 1:8-9; 6:1; II Thess. 3:14-15; I Tim. 5:19-21; Titus 3:1-5). Therefore, discipline in this church is governed by the following principles:

1. Church members who willfully absent themselves from the regular services for a period of three consecutive months or withhold their financial support for the same period of time, are subject to suspension from membership and corresponding privileges.
2. Unscriptural conduct or departure from the tenets of faith held by this church will be considered sufficient grounds upon which any person may be disqualified as a church member.

Unscriptural conduct necessary for church disciplinary action includes, but is not limited to:

- divisiveness
- immorality
- violence
- carnality
- drunkenness
- idolatry
- extortion
- heresy
- insubordination
- and the like.

3. The correct procedure for church discipline is described in Mt. 18:16-20; Rom. 16:17-18; I Cor. 2:6; II Thess. 3:12. Those Scriptures indicate that the following steps should be taken:

   a. The offending individual should be approached, initially by the one who has been offended, and they should strive to achieve a private reconciliation.
   b. If reconciliation is not achieved, then two or three others (especially pastors and elders) should meet with both parties and seek to achieve reconciliation.
   c. If reconciliation is not made at this point, the matter should be brought before all of the pastors and/or the church council and then, if necessary, before the entire church.
   d. The offending member who refuses to be reconciled should then be separated from the fellowship of the church until there

is repentance and reconciliation.

e. When there is repentance and reconciliation it should be confirmed by the pastors and/or the church council, and the separated person may then be welcomed back into membership and fellowship.

SECTION 2
Mutual Responsibility

This entire Article, dealing with membership and discipline, is based on the premise that all of the members of the church, along with its pastors and leaders, have a duty to care for each other, to admonish and exhort each other in the Lord, and to preserve the integrity, purity and unity of the church. Entering into membership in this church means entering into a covenant to minister to each other's spiritual needs. None are excluded from this duty. Note also that each new church member enters into this covenant by mutual consent with the whole church. A member cannot therefore disengage himself from the covenant unilaterally, but only with the consent or by the determination of the church (acting through its leaders).

SECTION 3
Resignation of Members

In harmony with the above, a church member cannot resign from membership simply to avoid church discipline. Resignation from membership does not become effective until it is accepted by the pastors and/or the church council. However, except where matters of discipline are involved, the leadership may not willfully withhold that acceptance.

SECTION 4
Methods of Discipline

At the discretion of the Senior Pastor or his delegated representative, church discipline may take one or more of the following forms:

- exclusion from participation in the communion
- exclusion from any one or more of the meetings of the church
- suspension of fellowship with the other members of the church
- dismissal from membership, either temporarily or permanently, along with the loss of all the privileges of membership

ARTICLE VII
BENEVOLENCE FUND POLICY

Vision Christian Church International, in the exercise of its religious purposes and missions, has established a benevolence fund to assist persons in financial need. The church welcomes contributions to the fund. Donors may feel free to suggest beneficiaries of the fund, or of their contribution to the fund. However, the administration of the funds, including all disbursements, is subject to the exclusive control and discretion of the Church Council. The Church Council may consider suggested designations, but, in no event is it bound to honor them. Donors wishing to make contributions subject to these conditions ordinarily may deduct their contributions from their taxable income if they itemize their deductions. Checks should be made payable to the church, with a notation that the funds are to be placed in the benevolence fund.

ARTICLE VIII
ORDINATION OF MINISTERS

SECTION 1
The Purpose of Ordination

1. This church, through and by its overseers, has the right to ordain, license, or otherwise credential Christian workers and ministers.
2. The purposes of ordination are to assist in attaining the goals of the church as set forth in the Bylaws and in this Chapter; to give legal and Scriptural authority to the ministries of the church; to establish sound doctrine; to encourage the upgrading of ministerial standards; and to provide the education and experience necessary to equip the potential minister.

SECTION 2
Two Classes of Credentials
There are two classes of credentials:

1. Licensed Minister. This may be issued following a stated period of training and instruction. The license authorized an individual to fulfill certain ministry functions, such as preaching, teaching, and counseling but without being classified as one of the ministry-gifts as recorded in Eph. 4:11-12. A licensed minister is expected to

function as a member of the ministry team in a local church, and should normally be under the authority of a fully ordained minister.

2. Ordained Minister. Ordination recognizes the development of the ministry-gift of an apostle, prophet, evangelist, pastor, or teacher (Eph. 4:11-12). An ordained pastor is expected to fulfill all of the duties of a minister of the gospel of Jesus Christ and of a shepherd of the flock of God (Acts 20:28-29; II Tim. 4:1-5), taking leadership of the church with authority tempered by humility and the grace of Christ (I Peter 5:2-4).

GENERAL ADMINISTRATION

I. TITLE: Associate Minister - Administration

II. PURPOSE:

   a. To supervise, give overall direction to, or to perform the various administrative and management functions of the church;
   b. To take particular responsibility for those departments that are subordinate to you; and
   c. To fulfill such other pastoral, teaching, and ministry duties as the call of God and the need of the church may require.

III. SCOPE: Under the Senior Minister, and Co-pastor, you have full authority in the church, and the right to attend the meetings, councils, etc., of every department, to influence their policies and decisions, and, if necessary, veto anything you judge to be against the policy of the Senior Minister or of the church; except that discretion will naturally be required when dealing with areas that are under the direct control of those who occupy your level on the flow chart.

Most of the areas of responsibility outlined below are also those of the senior minister, at least in their broad application; therefore a close working relationship with the Senior Minister must be maintained.

IV. AREAS OF RESPONSIBILITY:

A. Supervision

B. Co-ordination
C. Management
D. Properties
E. Bible College
F. Bible Fellowships
G. General Ministry
H. Special Projects

V. SPECIFIC DUTIES IN EACH AREA:

A. Supervision
1. To guide, assist, supervise, and where necessary direct, all the people involved in various activities in the church, especially in those departments that are specifically subordinate to you.

Standard: your ability to fulfill this task is recognized by the people, so that they turn to you for counsel, direction and guidance, and yield cheerfully to your leadership.

2. Whenever possible to delegate leadership of each department to a gifted person, and thereafter to be available yourself primarily as a resource person, counselor, coordinator, facilitator, or whatever capacity is necessary to achieve the smooth function and professional performance of each department. Key leaders, of course, are to be appointed only with the approval of the senior Pastor.

Standard: successful leadership is established in each department, and the various functions of the church are being properly and fruitfully fulfilled.

B. Co-ordination

To co-ordinate the various departments and activities in the church, plus the use of the buildings, facilities, and equipment; to achieve the best employment of our human and financial resources; to endeavor to anticipate and avoid potential conflicts.

Standard: a general unity and prosperity pervades the church, and no essential function is missing or ineffective.

C. Management

To give general oversight to, or to perform, the various administrative requirements of the church, including running the accountancy department, preparing the balance sheets and budgets, supervising the collection and banking of all monies, managing the fiscal and material resources of the church, and supervising the various sections of our office block.

Standard: those requiring office space should be provided for, to insure harmony is maintained between the various office staff. The resources of the church are being wisely and responsibly used.

D. Properties

To oversee the cleaning, maintenance, and repair of the building; to oversee the maintenance and repair of all the equipment used in the church, in its various departments, and in the office; to ensure that the image of the church is not harmed by a damaged, dirty, untidy, or unkempt appearance.

Standard: the cleanliness, beauty, and well-kept appearance of the church, its offices, and its equipment, are being maintained.

E. Bible College

To be responsible for the administrative aspects of our association with Vision, namely, the various reports, fees, collections, remittances, student rolls and records, etc, that are required of us; to teach from time to time in the College; to interview and counsel students; to fulfill the general responsibilities of a dean until a dean is appointed; and in general to ensure that the college program is administered effectively.

Standard: the requirements of Vision are being satisfied, the college is being satisfactorily maintained, and the needs of the student body are being met.

F. Bible Fellowships

To supervise the director of our Bible Fellowships, particularly to ensure:

(a) that the administrative requirements of the program are being fulfilled (submission of reports, statistics, etc); (b) that the program is running according to the policies that have been established; (c) that new contacts, visitors, and the like, are being properly referred either to the Director or to the Bible Fellowships leaders.

Standard: the Bible Fellowship program is being fully implemented and is fulfilling its appointed role in the church.

G. General Ministry

To be obedient to the call of God in your life to preach and teach the Word of God, as often as time and opportunity allow; to provide a strong example to the people of Christian leadership; to be an example in prayer, faith, and godliness; to counsel, minister, and in whatever way possible bring the healing of Christ to those who are hurting; in conjunction with all of the above items, and not to their detriment, to pursue an ongoing study of church administration and of theology and ministry.

Standard: your leadership, ministry, and Christ-like character are recognized, respected, and honored by the church, and you are committed to specific study projects.

H. Special Projects

To be available to handle special projects, when they are mutually agreeable.

Standard: agreement to fulfill a special project is not unreasonably withheld, and projects that are undertaken are brought to a successful conclusion.

VI. WORKING RELATIONSHIPS

1. Report to the Senior Pastor and work with him to find the will of God for the church and to implement the divine purpose.
2. Obtain reports from and give co-operative direction to the leaders of the various departments in the church, especially those who are directly subordinate to you.
3. Maintain your position on the Church Council, working closely with the Council Members and with the Senior Minister to implement the policies of the church.

YOUTH LEADER
Accountable to Pastor

RESPONSIBILITIES:
1. Responsible for direction of the teens' class on Friday evenings.
   a. Provide information, lectures, tapes, activities to motivate desire to be Christ-like.
   b. Provide activities and outings of fun, and songs.
   c. Collect and make $ for special projects.
      1) Set up bookkeeping system for your own records to compare with church statements.

2. Plan ahead a general schedule, Christmas, Valentines, etc. Check general schedule. Clear all outings with Overseer and parents. Submit schedule to Leadership meeting.
3. You are directly responsible for any questions, problems, etc. If a conflict arises do not ignore it. See parents, see Overseer - keep everything in the open with ministry staff.
4. Report all serious emotional problems to Overseer or Pastor. (i.e., suicide, abortion, drugs.)
5. Be Holy Spirit led, teach Biblical standards and principles. Help them to stand in the evil day.
6. Attend leadership meetings.
7. Choose curriculum for each class - be prepared.
8. Encourage and continue preparation for class lesson before Sunday morning.
9. See guide for other coordinators.

CHILDREN'S CHURCH
Supervisor
Accountable to Leadership
Direct all children's activities in Vision, coordinating activities smoothly within each department. Encourage and train teaching staff. Includes Sunday School, Nursery, Youth, and all areas involving younger people.

DUTIES:

1. Order all supplies through Board approval and voucher system. Determine costs of departmental needs.
2. Teach the class coordinators how to enforce discipline:

    a. Unruly behavior should be corrected verbally, it is unlawful to strike a child that is not your own.

    b. You may show displeasure in your voice, but never berate a child.

    c. Remember to correct behavior by instruction.

    d. Do all to keep the child in the room, he cannot learn if he has been removed. However, if he continually disrupts the class, take him to an usher.

    e. Make certain that the parent is informed why the child was expelled from the class.

    f. Any guest speaker is to be approved before they are allowed to speak. Outside speakers (not members of Vision) will submit a resume for approval.

3. Substitutes are to be approved by you before they take the class.
4. Establish general curriculum. Evaluate textbooks and methods of teaching.
5. Have a substitute in mind for emergencies (May occasionally use an approved video).
6. Assure adequate preparation for all classes.
7. Display leadership to other instructors. Maintain good relationships with all persons (staff, congregation, etc.)
8. Stay ahead of the staff in vision to keep everyone on the road to reach their goals.
9. Delegate to the Coordinator of each department the assignment to schedule teachers – one completed copy to be given to the prospective teacher by the last week of the previous month, one copy to be submitted at the leadership meeting.
10. Appointment of any Coordinator must be cleared by Leadership.
11. Report all serious problems to Leadership.
12. Assure that no teacher misses more than one out of every 5 services. This includes illnesses. Schedules must be adjusted accordingly.

GOALS: Get them involved in plays, skits, and teaching programs. Have regular performances for church services with scriptures or music. Increase resources and ideas. Host a teaching for parents on child discipline. Keep records to be compiled for a book to help service smaller churches and/or seminars.

OTHER DUTIES:

1. Coordinate special seminars.
2. Arrange for special music, plays, summer Bible school.
3. Evaluate and encourage those working under you.
4. Reward teachers for their efforts with banquets, plaques.

SKILLS AND REQUIREMENTS:

1. Be a teacher, able to impart the Word into the life of a child.
2. Be able to organize and manage.
3. Be compatible and compassionate.
4. Acquire Biblical training and skill with the Word.
5. Be open to the leading of the Holy Spirit.
6. Portray Godly characteristics as an example for students.
7. Demonstrate teaching skills, creativity and vision.
8. Integrity, a tither, loyal to the vision of Vision Christian Fellowship.
9. Use the gifts of encouragement for those working with you.
10. Build a team on the understanding of one another's strengths.
11. "Pull up" the person behind you.
12. Help others to know how to pull someone else up.
13. Deal with strife immediately.
14. Delegate the changes in the Bulletin Boards in the Children's church area. Change monthly. Keep them vital and interesting.
15. Make a yearly calendar with a suggested plan, to submit to the monthly leadership meetings.

Children's Church COORDINATORS and Teachers:
Principle function: Teach children in the way they should go in accordance with God's word, training them with love and discipline.

1. To lead, teach, train, establish, develop, cultivate and mature the children until they are able to duplicate in others the same attitudes.
2. To produce in the youth a devout spirit, full of praise and faith.
3. To instill in the youth a desire to know and to memorize the Word of God.
4. To develop programs, awards, rewards, etc. that will inspire diligent study.
5. To be positive, outgoing and convincing.
6. See youth guidelines.

DUTIES:
1. Observe various methods of teaching and learn how to use them in the classroom.
2. Attend all Children's Church teacher meetings.
    a. Review and discuss methods of upgrading and improving teaching. Using a mutual exchange of ideas and opinions.
    b. Have parties and get together for appreciation.
3. Listen to all service tapes of sermons missed and keep current with the teaching of the membership. (A free tape will be provided for each teacher the day he/she works.)
4. Collect monies from each class, teaching on the blessings of stewardship.
    a. Count $ and deposit in marked tithe envelope in sanctuary.
    b. Use for your own projects, adopted kids etc...
5. Plan ahead for general schedule (Thanksgiving, special events) and make your needs known to supervisor.
6. Be responsible for communication with the parents.
7. You are directly responsible to the Children's Church Coordinator. You are accountable for any questions, problems, etc. If a conflict arises do not ignore it. See parents, see overseer - keep everything in the open with ministry staff.
8. Be Holy Spirit led.
9. Love the children and minister to them with the gifts of the Spirit.
10. Learn songs for ministry to the adult body.
11. Have fun, and demonstrate that the JOY of the Spirit is God-Given gifts to us all.
12. Remember that discipline is training that develops self-control - never spanking.
    a. The teacher must relate any discipline problems with the proper parents. Keep them informed.
    b. Disorderly children are to be sent to the usher in charge and they are to be observed and "contained" by the usher at the back of the auditorium until the service concludes. They are not to disrupt the service by returning to the parents. Be certain that a report is given to the parent after service.
13. Do not allow unsanctioned helpers (i.e., older kids trying to escape the service). A minimum number of teachers in each class, please.
14. Pray and set aside time to study prior to coming to class.
15. Do all copy work prior to pre-service prayer.

16. Keep kids out of the office, it is off limits.

REQUIREMENTS:
1. Must have the desire to teach and impart God's Word into the life of a child.
2. Must be compatible, yet able to maintain order.
3. Must portray Godly characteristics as an example.

GOALS:
To possibly have special outreaches into schools or public.

NURSERY MINISTRY
Coordinator: REPORTS TO CHILDREN'S CHURCH SUPERVISOR
It is a reward to serve the people of God and it will benefit you and uplift the ministry of Vision Christian Church International to love the babies of our families. This is an essential ministry that must be provided for. These little people are vitally important to the LORD.

DUTIES:
1. To delegate authority to others.
2. To schedule nursery supervision for all regular and special events.
3. Give instruction to how to better teach infants.
4. To hold necessary meetings to instruct.

NURSERY TEACHERS:
1. Create meetings of fun with occasional projects, awards, and approved treats.
2. Think of new ideas that will benefit the nursery ministry.
3. Remember that discipline is training which develops self-control - never spanking.
4. Attend all seminars and meetings that could enrich your teaching abilities.
5. Play pleasant Christian music during the class period, or the service may be listened to if the time is right.
6. Let your needs be known to the Children's Church Coordinator.
7. Arrive on time to open this room and be prepared for the arrival of the infants.
8. Provide care for Fundamentals class.
9. Do not allow unsanctioned helpers, all older kids (not scheduled to work) should be in the Children's Church or in the Sanctuary.

a. Encourage all parents to return to the Sanctuary, allowing assigned worker to care for the children.

b. Nursing mothers may come in, and also assigned assistants (such as particular teenage girls that desire to minister in this area).

c. The nursery leader is in charge, an assistant is to help.

d. We are a family of FAITH, and we love one another in the Spirit.

10. Make certain that all belongings of a child are marked, this includes diapers, bags, bottles, blankets, etc. Have all belongings taken home after each service.

11. If you do not know the child's name, place masking tape with the name on his back and call him by name, remembering that a child knows his name.

12. Children are never to be left unattended, there are NO EXCUSES. THE WORD IS NEVER.

13. You are required to listen to any service messages you miss. A free tape will be provided for the staff.

14. Parents are to pick up their children within 15 minutes of the close of the service. There is no need to be rude if they do not come back, just pray for them and then kindly relate to the parent again concerning the time limit. Thank you for your attention and love.

15. You are responsible for the condition of the classroom. You should be in before pre-service prayer to make certain the chairs are in order and the atmosphere set. After class, please return chairs and have children assist in picking up garbage, scissors, and so on.

GOALS: Make this a self-sufficient ministry. Write up guidelines on how to set up a successful nursery and cause it to prosper. Have the latest equipment available for infants and children.

REMEMBER: The nursery slogans: the only thing constant is change! Or we shall not all sleep, but we will all be changed.

MUSIC MINISTRY
Accountable to the Pastor

The key word is to "flow" with no in-between-song talking and no abrupt change in key and song type. The anointing of the Holy Spirit must guide the song selections. It is important that we present ourselves in a professional agenda. The Music Team should pray together prior to service time, and stand by ready before the service begins.

1. A CALL TO WORSHIP will be accomplished by the Worship Leader. OPENING THE SERVICE: These are all to be assigned by the Worship Leaders.
   a. A hymn will normally begin the service.
   b. The Worship team will come forward with a snappy opening song.
   c. The vision or confession will be recited.
   d. An appropriate jubilant scripture verse will be read.
   e. Followed by a vibrant prayer.
   f. Listen to the Holy Spirit for ideas as to how to begin a power-packed service.
2. It is of utmost importance that each service begins with an enthusiastic, warm, and exciting unity of worship.
3. The welcome must be fast, and moving so we do not cool down.
4. The Worship leader controls the praise service in order to usher the congregation into the presence of God, the Gifts of the Spirit, and the hearing of the Word.
5. Always confer with the person in charge to see if there is a specific topic to continue and then determine line up by prayer.
6. The Worship Team leads and causes the service to start on time.
7. Prepares a separate list of the line up for the drummer and the sound man.
8. Will assign one special per week, can be done by a group or solo along with or in addition to the choir.
9. No talking and joking on the platform, go up together in an orderly and enthusiastic manner.
10. Plan rehearsal schedule to maximize time and talent and accomplish goals.
11. Select and encourage all members of the Music Team to come forth with their best abilities.
12. Select Music Team on the basis of their music ability and their hearts toward the Lord.
13. Make the song selections varied enough to minister to the needs of the entire congregation, regardless of age or ethnic background.

14. Supervise the unity of the team, looking for quality worship and music. Develop a team spirit.
15. Prepare a monthly and yearly schedule.
16. Coordinate all areas of vocal music.
17. Train musicians, hold classes, practices.
18. Plan get-togethers for praise and fun. Look for reasons and excuses to praise God with music and involve others, such as "it's spring" or whatever.
19. Give rewards and awards for special work.
20. Assign director for Choir.
21. Check with visiting ministries to find out what they want during altar calls, etc...
22. Teach all members of the music section about Worship, including techniques, Song of the Lord, flowing in the Spirit, etc. Be certain there is a unity of purpose and desire in these areas.
23. Order music, tapes, etc. It is necessary to have current songs.
24. Have team sit forward and be ready to go.

Other duties:

1. Arrange and prepare for the team ministry in other congregations, with Leadership approval.
2. Arrange special music for all Vision events and weddings.
3. Increase musical skills.

REQUIREMENTS:

1. Have a proven ministry.
2. Obtaining biblical training to be skilled in the Word.
3. Have leadership, integrity, talent and skill.
4. Desire to be led by the Holy Spirit and flexible enough to move toward that goal.
5. Be in total unity with the leadership, in one accord. Bring every conflict to solution prior to service beginning.
6. Be faithful to set an example of seeking God, and having His mind for the service. It is your responsibility to KNOW how to direct this portion of the service.

GOALS:

1. To host music seminars.
2. To develop signing ministries, and special groups that minister.
3. To obtain equipment to record quality music and song.
4. To raise up artists and songsters from within the body.
5. To encourage banner making.

MUSIC SCHEDULE

DATE:_____

Praise/Worship Songs:
    Key?

_____
_____
_____
_____
_____

Singers/Musicians (with instruments):

_____
_____
_____
_____
_____

Special Music:

_____
Song:_____
_____
Song:_____
_____

Pre-Service Music:

_____
_____

Music for Healing Line:

_____
_____

Music as church is dismissed:

_____

_____

SPECIALS AND SOLOS
Accountable to: Music Minister

Standards will be set to encourage the able and restrict others so that the anointing of God may be released upon the congregation. Vision feels that music is a primary way to allow the congregation to center upon the Lord and allow us to be of one mind and accord.

1. Those who do not preach before singing will be heard again.
2. You may explain the song, or give a brief testimonial, but do not preach, someone else is waiting to do that! You have been asked to minister in song, so sing with anointing and smile when you are finished.
3. Keep the flow. Extreme styles of music would not be appropriate for Sunday morning service. Keep the radical styles for parties and fun times.
4. Be properly dressed, (neat and modest, no shorts or bare feet. No tight clothes, please).
5. Pray beforehand.
6. Clear with the music minister and the sound man prior to the service.
7. Prepare with accompanist before service.
8. Be ready in the sanctuary 15 minutes before service begins in case there are any last minute questions.
9. The words of the song must be scripturally correct. The music should convey joy, enthusiasm, triumph, deliverance, expectancy, or reverence.
10. Be seated close to the platform in order for you to be available without pause in the flow.
11. If you make a mistake, quietly continue to praise God and continue without apology.

BAND AND WORSHIP TEAM (own initiative)

To work with the band leader, the musicians, and the worship team, assisting them wherever desired or possible, and encouraging them to play, sing, and minister in the unity and anointing of the Spirit so that their impact on the worship services is maximized.

Standard: the band maintains a good balance of sound between each instrument, and also in relation to the worship of the people; the singers are efficiently organized and enhance the singing of the congregation; the band members and singers maintain a loving relationship with each other.

CHOIRS AND SOLOISTS (act with approval)

To develop various singing ensembles and soloists to minister in each of our public services, including the presentation each year of two or three major productions.

Standard: a choir and other smaller ensembles are established, and sing regularly and effectively; soloists are found and encouraged to sing; a major production is presented from time to time, probably at special seasons such as Easter and Christmas.

DANCE AND DRAMA (act with approval)

To develop the use of dance and drama in the church, through special productions, and where appropriate, as an adjunct to an ordinary worship service.

Standard: those who are skilled in dance and drama are found and encouraged to participate, and these two expressions of the arts in worship are a regular part of the ministry of the church.

SOUND DEPARTMENT
Accountable to Leadership

1. Arrive at station 30 minutes before the meeting.
2. Position and check all microphones.
    a. Eliminate feedback screeches and check controls for changes.
    b. Set predetermined sound levels.
    c. Balance speakers and instruments as directed.

3. Play soft worship music before service, so it will be a pleasant, soothing environment for study and prayer. Or have musicians play softly.
4. Keep stock of blank audio tapes handy for the message.
5. Deliver wireless microphone to speaker if available or necessary.
6. Be invisible in your job, do not attract attention to yourself.
7. Recruit helpers that will do exactly as directed.
8. Label master tape with appropriate title, if one is not directed by speaker.
9. Accommodate soloists who use pre-recorded tapes, have tapes prepared and ready.
10. Practice and know what the musicians want, and do that!
11. Purchase batteries for mikes, picks for guitars.
12. Be in charge of the care of church owned instruments.
13. This job entails technique and artistry. He is a participant in the worship service and must be a worshipper.
14. Exemplary participation in services is expected. He is under observation.
15. Keep an eye on the person in charge, or the person leading the song for needed corrections. The leader must be heard above the instruments.
16. Accommodate visiting ministries, be hospitable and cooperative.
17. This job requires tact and diplomacy, cannot be frustrated.

TAPE MINISTRY
Accountable to Pastor

DUTIES: Leader

1. Assign someone to duplicate tapes after each service.
2. Advise secretary well in advance of low supply.
3. All masters must be stored with secretary in office desk where you can have access, not in sanctuary. Deposit every week. *important.
4. Duplicate tapes should be promptly distributed to the person requesting them.
5. All payment for tapes should be in advance.
6. Any tapes to be mailed out should be so labeled. Please assign someone to mail out tapes.

7. Provide free tapes for all Children's Church teachers of classes held during that particular service time. This is a service provided to the active staff only.
8. Money from tapes should be placed in a labeled envelope and placed in the tithe box.
9. Provide free tape for all new visitors.

GOALS: To have local series tapes displayed in professional packaging for sale. To expand the tape duplication system with plug-in modules.

EXECUTIVE SECRETARY

I. TITLE: Executive Secretary

II. PURPOSE: To manage and co-ordinate all of the various activities associated with the church office; to fulfill the duties of private secretary to the senior minister.

III. SCOPE: Under the senior minister, co-pastor, and associate minister, you have authority over all matters connected with management of the office, use of the church and office equipment, the church calendar, access to our facilities, and to the telephones.

IV. AREAS OF RESPONSIBILITY:

    A. Management.
    B. Development.
    C. Secretarial.
    D. Clerical.
    E. Ministry.
    F. Special Projects.

V. SPECIFIC DUTIES IN EACH AREA:

A. Management

To provide daily management of the church office and its various tasks; to note and report any inefficiency or inadequacy in office procedures or equipment; to maintain supplies of all necessary items; to supervise volunteer or paid help working in the office.

Standard: the office is functioning smoothly and efficiently, fulfilling its required tasks on time and to the benefit of the church.

B. Development

To develop ways to improve our office procedures and to utilize better our various mailing and statistical lists; to solicit lay volunteers to help in the office; to prepare the way for additional paid office staff; to maintain an atmosphere of faith and vision in the office.

Standard: a sense of creativity, of growth, of faith, of advance, of love and unity in the Holy Spirit characterizes our office and its staff, both paid and volunteer.

C. Secretarial

To act as private secretary for the senior pastor, attending to his correspondence, telephone calls, and the other tasks that are usual for a private secretary. The requirements of this position are to take precedence over all other tasks that fall within the secretary's responsibility. Work may be done for other people, but only by the secretary's own consent, and not to the detriment of work of their duty to the senior minister.

Standard: the senior minister is satisfied that his requirements are being met.

D. Clerical

To perform, or supervise the performance of, several clerical functions, namely: (a) banking on time the various monies collected by the church each week; (b) computerizing the details of money donors, new visitors, converts, water baptisms, and other necessary or useful statistics; (c) handle the various mailings that are required from time to time; (d) ensure that visitors, enquirers, telephone callers, trades people, and the like, are dealt with pleasantly and courteously; (e) co-ordinate and control the church calendar.

Standard: the stated clerical tasks are adequately fulfilled; the calendar is functioning so that event clashes are avoided; and all who have a valid need to use our facilities have reasonable access to them.

E. Ministry

To treat your position as a ministry, not merely a job, and hence be available to offer basic counsel to people who visit or phone; to be obedient to the larger call of God in your life, in prayer, faith, teaching of the Word, and ministering Christ to people.

Standard: the people recognize you, not just as a secretary, but as a vital part of our ministry-team, gifted by Christ, and serving Him.

F. Special Projects

To be available to handle special projects, when they are mutually agreeable, and approved by the senior pastor.

Standard: agreement to fulfill a special project is not unreasonably withheld, and the project is successfully completed.

VI. WORKING RELATIONSHIPS

1. You are answerable to the senior minister, then to the associate minister, then to the assistant minister, but not to any others.
2. You should offer all reasonable courtesy and co-operation to all who are in leadership in the church, and indeed to anyone who has a justifiable expectation of assistance and ministry from the church office.

SECRETARY GOALS

1. *"...he that ruleth, (let him do it) with diligence..."* (Rom. 12:8)

2. Automate church office procedures utilizing computer equipment.

ACCOUNTING/BUDGET GOALS

"...he that ruleth, (let him do it) with diligence..." (Rom. 12:8)

1. Develop a complete budget system for Vision Christian Church International, by line item.
2. Automate completely an audit trail system.
3. Supervise independent audit of financial records.

SECRETARY
Accountable to the Pastor
The function of the secretary is to provide services for the pastor and the church office.

1. Provide secretarial functions such as typing, ordering.
2. Organize office procedures and duties.
3. Coordinate records between departments.
4. Be responsible for inventory and ordering of supplies.
5. Oversee public relations of the telephone, be friendly.
6. Cause the office to run smoothly, in the love of God.
7. Type all prophecies that are given, for filing.
8. Coordinate records for monthly, quarterly, yearly or special reports.
9. Supervise others in office.
10. Oversees bulletin boards in sanctuary, assuring they are current.
11. Coordinate room usage and schedules.
12. Files.
13. Schedule counseling appointments for a.m. only.
14. Keep addresses in order.
15. Maintain order and neatness of office, keep inventory of supplies and keep stock current.
16. Organize and cause workday efficiency.
17. Get mail, make deposit as required.
18. Attend Leadership meetings and type up detailed minutes in an outline format.
19. Write a follow up visitor letter for every new comer, followed up by a phone call.
20. Make copies for departments as requested.
21. Prepare monthly calendar for distribution each month.

REQUIREMENTS:
Office skills, organization and management skills, integrity,
confidentiality, ability to get along with others, dedication, loyalty, a
servant's heart.

BOOKSTORE
Accountable to Leadership

1. Be responsible for the operation of the bookstore, (opening and closing, locking register etc.).
2. Account for weekly receipts, make deposits, keep a record of all receipts and disbursements.
3. Order books, videos, cassettes, gift items as necessary.
4. Making yearly or bi-yearly inventory.
5. Display items attractively, with signs for promotions.
6. Write to companies about products and catalogs, and keep record of correspondence.
7. Sow books into our sister churches or other designated ministries as the Lord leads.
8. Train others to help man the bookstore.

SECRETARY/OFFICE MANAGER

I. TITLE: Church Secretary

II. PURPOSE: To manage and co-ordinate all of the various activities associated with the church office; to fulfill the duties of private secretary to the senior pastor.

III. SCOPE: Under the senior pastor, associate pastor, and assistant pastor, the church secretary has authority over all matters connected with the management of the office, use of church and office equipment, the church calendar, access to our facilities, to the telephones, and the like.

IV. AREAS OF RESPONSIBILITY:
    A. Management.
    B. Development.
    C. Secretarial.
    D. Clerical.
    E. Ministry.
    F. Special Projects.

V. SPECIFIC DUTIES IN EACH AREA:

    A. Management

To provide daily management of the church office and its various tasks; to note and report any inefficiency or inadequacy in office procedures or equipment; to maintain supplies of all necessary items to supervise volunteer or paid help working in the office.

The Standard to Be Reached: the office is functioning smoothly and efficiently, fulfilling its required tasks on time and to the benefit of the church.

B. Development

To develop ways to improve our office procedures and to utilize better our various mailing and statistical lists; to solicit lay volunteers to help in the office; to prepare the way for additional paid office staff; to maintain an atmosphere of faith and vision in the office.

The Standard to Be Reached: a sense of creativity, of growth, of faith, of advance, of love and unity in the Holy Spirit characterizes our office and its staff, both paid and volunteer.

C. Secretarial

To act as private secretary for the senior pastor, attending to his correspondence, telephone calls, and the other tasks that are usual for a private secretary. The requirements of this position are to take precedence over all other tasks that fall within the secretary's responsibility. Work may be done for other people, but only by the secretary's own consent, and not to the detriment of work required by the senior pastor.

The Standard to Be Reached: the senior pastor is satisfied that his requirements are being met.

D. Clerical

To perform, or supervise the performance of, several clerical functions, namely: (a) banking on time the various monies collected by the church each week; (b) computerizing the details of money donors, new visitors, converts, water baptisms, and other necessary or useful statistics; (c) handle the various mailings that are required from time to time; (d) ensure that visitors, enquirers, telephone callers, trades people, and the like, are dealt with pleasantly and courteously; (e) co-ordinate and control the church calendar.

The Standard To Be Reached: the stated clerical tasks are adequately fulfilled; the calendar is functioning so that event clashes are avoided; and all who have a valid need to use our facilities have reasonable access to them.

E. Ministry

To treat your position as a ministry, not merely a job, and hence be available to offer basic counsel to people who visit or phone; to be obedient to the larger call of God in your life, in prayer, faith, teaching of the Word, and pastoring Christ to people.

Part of this larger task will be to shield the pastors from unnecessary phone calls, by handling as many basic or minor problems as practicable - yet always with discretion and kindness, and never conveying an impression that the people or their problems are unimportant.

The Standard to Be Reached: the people recognize the secretary, not just as a clerk, but as a vital part of our ministry-team, gifted by Christ, and serving Him.

F. Special Projects

To be available to handle special projects, when they are mutually agreeable, and approved by the senior pastor.

The Standard To Be Reached: agreement to fulfill a special project is not unreasonably withheld, and the project is successfully completed.

VI. WORKING RELATIONSHIPS

1. The secretary is answerable to the senior pastor, then to the associate pastor, then to the assistant pastor, but not to any others.

2. The secretary must offer all reasonable courtesy and co-operation to all who are in leadership in the church, and indeed to anyone

who has a justifiable expectation of assistance and ministry from the church office.

ASSISTANT TO THE TREASURER
Counting service contributions
Accountable to Treasurer

1. The job to count money is absolutely confidential and done privately.
2. You will not reveal amounts of individual giving to ANYONE not on ministerial staff.
3. You are not to discuss who gives and who does not.
4. You make copies of the blank forms which are kept filed in the office.
5. Please accurately record all contributions on contribution record form.
6. There must be a minimum of two counters approved by a member of the Board of Directors.

ELDER/OVERSEER/LEADER There are several words used in the scripture to explain the word elder: Zagen, siyb, episkopos, epesdopoa, supresbuteros, pressbuteros. There is no account of the origin of elder, but the book of Acts seems to imply that this function was clearly understood by all.

Elders are always plural in number.[10] Elders help carry the weight of the responsibility of leading God's people. Elders have specific functions and responsibilities which may differ.

Jesus, as the Head of the Church, equips the church with leadership. There must be one person anointed of God to make the final decisions for each local assembly, this is the Senior Pastor or Presiding Elder. Without this leadership there is confusion and chaos. One person must bear the weight of the ultimate and final decisions in given expression of believers.

Ideally Vision Christian Church International should have a plurality of elderships, with one Elder, the Senior Pastor, directing the Deacons and congregation. This plurality does not necessarily mean that all function at

---

[10] When understood as the Pastor's five-fold ministry within a locality.

the same level of responsibility or influence or are due the same honor. (I Tim. 5:17)

God places more emphasis on character and integrity rather than charisma. All the laborers in Vision must be divinely appointed and called. No degree of education can make a person effective without the call of God. The character qualifications of I Tim. 3:2 and Titus 1:6 are to be ones possessed or being acquired by those in leadership.

The most important area of ministry is that of hearing the voice of God, and then communicating to the congregation what God has spoken. It is of no value unless it is communicated and understood by the flock. The Pastor & Leadership Team will lead the congregation, proving to be examples to the flock. Jesus was our prime example.

Leaders are expected to learn about management and leadership techniques. They must be an active, involved member of Vision Christian Church International, and a regular tither.

ELDERS/LEADERS JOB DESCRIPTION
The Elders/Leaders assist the Pastor with the spiritual oversight of the church. The main function of the leaders is that they rule (Heb. 13:7, I Thess. 5:12).

Specific duties:

1. Love the people of Vision.
2. Serve the people.
3. Have the ability to teach the Word.
4. Help guard the flock of God and be on the lookout for strange and varied teachings that could pervert the truth.
5. Pray for the church and flock.
6. Help assume duties of correction and know the congregation. Spot potential conflict situations.
7. Let their gifts flow, and their strengths reign. Learn the gifts of the body and help develop them. (John 10:14)
8. Share ideas, problems and advise solutions.
9. Promote evangelism.
10. Build leadership and accountability in others.
11. Help pre-planning and scheduling.

12. Oversee and direct deacons.
13. They must know how to rule and lead and not "laud over" God's people.
14. Make regular contact with the body.
15. Give support to the various functions of the church.
16. Oversee all other departments, guiding, integrating and directing human efforts toward accomplishing specified tasks.
17. Leaders are to be sharp in appearance, and rule with dignity.
18. Leaders are to help minister, greet, and be accountable.
19. Leaders are expected to attend all services, coming 30 minutes early and staying after to minister and fellowship. In addition they are to attend pre-service.
20. Leaders are not elected by popular vote but appointed by the Senior Pastor with apostolic input. (Acts 20:28, 14:23) There is no reference to the length of a Leader's term in the Scriptures. Therefore, unless a person withdraws from this office, he remains an active leader indefinitely.

There needs to be a high level of unanimity amongst the leadership. The candidates must have exemplary leadership in ministry, cannot be novices, and must have a proven calling.

LEADERS' OVERSIGHT MEETINGS
Leaders are expected to attend regular meeting designed to establish goals. The goals of these meetings are:

1. To preserve the unity of the Spirit, one mind, one purpose, one voice and one judgment.
2. To learn to submit to one another.
3. To develop intimate relationship with each other.
4. To maintain honesty, transparency and open communication.
5. To develop a servant heart.
6. To edify one another.
7. To learn to be loyal to one another. To be committed to God's vision and to each other.
8. To be taught, reproved, corrected, and trained by the Word.
9. To be examples to one another, to have the same spirit. To learn to pray together. To not draw disciples after themselves, to have the mind of Christ.

QUALIFICATIONS: The candidates must have exemplary leadership of ministry, and not be novices. They must have a proven calling or ministerial gifting. They must be active, involved, punctual, tithers of Vision. They must be above reproach and qualify with Godly ability according to I Tim. 3:1-7, Titus 1:7-9.

MINISTERS ACCOUNTABLE TO LEADERSHIP

1. Ministers recognized at Vision will be those who qualified in this local body, or from those places whose doctrines and standards are equivalent. They will present a letter of recommendation. Newly arriving "ministers" will be evaluated. There will be a time of appraisement. Many will be given an opportunity to operate in their calling.
2. Ministers may officiate in the Communion, do baptisms and weddings (etc.) as qualified and as required.
3. Ministers will be a support network to the Leadership, and will not Kingdom-build for themselves.
4. Ministers will report directly to the Leadership. They will display irreproachable conduct and loyalty.
5. Ministers may meet with Leadership meetings as invited.

DEACONS

ACCOUNTABLE to an appointed Head Deacon who reports to a Leader.

Function: A deacon - male or female - or server as they are called in the New Testament, has many functions - serving in a practical way doing tasks for the church. They are to maintain Vision Christian Church International in operating order, distribute to the needs of the body in order to enable others to live in the realm of God's promises.

1. Church Facilities: Delegate the details
    a. Building appearance, maintenance and cleanliness.
    b. External appearance of facility kept in order as well.
    c. Ventilation and lighting.
    d. Take charge of all construction and painting.
    e. Obtaining and purchasing supplies needed to operate.
        1. A monthly inventory shall be made of needs.
        2. Supplies will be kept in stock (for cleaning and bathrooms).

f. Deacons will search for things that need attention, not waiting to be asked to do it.

2. Obtaining funds for projects.
   a. Building fund.
   b. Special projects.

3. Help the poor of the church membership.
   a. Purchase food.
   b. Help find employment.

4. Supervise ushers.
5. Attend leadership and deacon meetings.
6. Inventory and maintain the tools that belong to the church. They are not to be loaned out. Deacons may use the tools on outreach projects and return them immediately.
7. Determine financial aid given to the needy.
8. Distribute food that is gathered and stored.
9. Arrange for necessary transportation.
10. Help find or arrange for housing for the homeless, distressed, and visitors.
11. Help assist in funerals.
12. Project meeting future needs of the church.
13. Rally work parties, plan, motivate and initiate projects.
14. Lock and unlock the sanctuary, and turn on air conditioners sufficiently prior to service to cool off areas.
15. Order flowers or gifts for Vision for members in the hospital, (babies, etc.)
16. Prepare for Communion.
    a. Communion is not to be prepared during pre-service prayer.
    b. Communion is to be prepared by Deacons in a reverent manner, not by children.
    c. Deacons may serve communion and fellowship to those confined to bed with illness.
    d. Deacons clean up after communion service and store equipment.
    e. Deacons order needed supplies, i.e., cups, bread, wine/juice.

17. Deacons are to help with visitation.
   a. Visitation is a core of Pastoral Care.
   b. Deacons visit to determine needs in order that essential help may be assured.
   c. Deacons will relate those needs by calling upon those members of the congregation who are trained or experienced to meet the situation.
   d. There is to be a minimum of weekly visits to those members who are ill.
   e. Critically ill are visited two - three times a week.
   f. A goal to include those in good health to be visited bi-monthly.
   g. Care of Seniors is vital, and honor is due them. We must pursue the elderly and assure their care.
   h. Deacons may ask others to help with visitation.
18. Deacons submit monthly written reports to all areas of responsibility. Strict records are expected from this ministry because it entails so many activities.

Personal Requirements:

1. Must tithe, be faithful, committed and be loyal to Vision.
2. Must have a desire to serve others and meet needs.
3. Must have the ability to make others feel included, and to train them.
4. Show the love and mercy of God.
5. Have influence by encouraging and being an example. It is the wisdom of God to provide deacons to assist the eldership to serve the work of the ministry. A deacon's chief responsibility is to serve the Lord in the work of the Ministry.
6. Each deacon must exhibit a true serving spirit. One's character and calling will be tested before calling them into office. There may be a training time or an investigation time prior to choosing them. The office of deacon will not be used as a testing ground.
7. Deacons must be those willing to serve and not aspiring to personal gain or recognition. They will be committed to rally the body to meet the needs of the saints and to perform works of service. They will plan and motivate projects.
8. Deacons appoint new deacons, at their discretion, with Leadership approval.

USHERS
Accountable to Deacon in charge

The function of an usher is to be a "Porter" a guard or a watchman to maintain order in the church. The head usher will also be a deacon. Ushers maintain order, have charge of the furniture and equipment and enforce the rules and regulations of the church while the service is in progress. The doorkeeper is a very important ministry in the church. Each must be sensitive to the direction of the Spirit so as not to offend others while doing the job. Ushers are ambassadors for the church:

1. In a loving manner, maintain order in the service. Assume post inside sanctuary at the same time until the end of services.
    a. Do as instructed by the person in charge of the meeting.
    b. Be alert to handle disturbances, needs and problems.
    c. Be on guard to protect others.
    d. Keep order before and after service.
    e. Do not allow children to run around the building unattended at any time. (Speak to parents in a kind way.)
    f. Disorderly children are to be sent to the usher in charge and they are to be observed and "contained" by the usher at the back of the auditorium until the service concludes. They are not to disrupt the service by returning to the parents. Be certain that a report is given to the parent after service.
2. Greeters: The head usher oversees the Greeters which greet at the entry doors and dispel the feelings of disorientation.
    a. Greeters give each new visitor a brochure.
    b. Don't overwhelm them.
    c. Get their name and address put into the offering box.
    d. Try to introduce them to someone with a commonality.
    e. Hand all visitors a welcome packet. When visitors are acknowledged during service also give them (key ring, ink pen, etc.).
    f. Be pleasant, (use breath mints).
    g. A door Greeter need not function as an Usher, it may be two separate jobs.
    h. Door Greeters are to be on post 30 minutes before service begins and never leave duty without informing the head usher. Assist patrons by directing them to sanctuary, carry

Bibles, help them out of the rain, etc...
i. Have someone at outside entrance.
3. Ushers seat people, trying to fill up the front first, so the late comers can be seated without interrupting the flow of the service.
    a. Please do not seat people during prophetic times.
    b. Please do not allow anyone to traffic during these times. Teach the children to stay in the sanctuary. Do not let kids roam the building.
    c. Try to seat parents of small children near the cry room to avoid distractions.
    d. Keep all movement to a minimum during the giving of the Word.
4. Be prepared to collect an offering if required.
5. Certain appointed Ushers and Deacons are to be the "catchers" for the prayer line. No one is to minister here if they are not willing to receive ministry for themselves from time to time.
    a. Catchers must be invisible.
    b. Catchers must not divert the attention of the minister.
    c. Catchers are not to touch the person before catching.
6. Appoint overhead person to carefully check the music transparencies to assure they agree with the expected lineup, prior to the service beginning.
7. Be an information center for visitors.
8. Oversee lost and found.
9. Dismiss the Children's church back into the auditorium after service.
10. Hand out Bible before ministry of the Word, collect trash and straighten furniture at the end of the service.
11. Perform the duties of the Greeter for late patrons.
12. Post monthly Usher and Greeter assignments.
13. Dress neatly, look sharp, no shorts at the door.
14. Submit monthly schedule at Leadership meeting.
15. Ushers are not to be playing with their kids, reading books, or being distracted while on post.
16. Have get-togethers to promote team spirit.
17. Head Usher may promote and recruit others into the Ushers program (check with leadership).
18. If you are aware of any situation that needs attention, it is up to you to see it through. You have the authority. If you need help,

ask for it.

   a. Awareness - Have knowledge of what is going on around you.

   b. Vigilance - Know how to act (not react), don't close your eyes.

   c. Expect the unexpected - Do not be caught off guard.

   d. Pride - In your church and in your job. Be the best! Be professional. Lead by example.

19. Ushers are to stock tithe envelopes and put them in the sanctuary at regular intervals.
20. Ushers must copy and maintain a ready stock of "Welcome Brochures" for the visitors. Carefully keep master copy on file in the office.
21. Ushers will be called upon to deliver messages and forms to various members.
22. YOU SHOULD BE KNOWN AS THE "LOVE SQUAD" BECAUSE YOU WILL CAUSE PEOPLE TO FEEL COMFORTABLE, WELCOME, AND BRING A SENSE OF ORDER TO THE SERVICE.

REQUIREMENTS: Dependability, leadership, integrity, humility. A desire to allow the fruit of the Spirit to operate at all times. To be prompt and alert.

SINGLES LEADERS
Accountable to Elders
Singles are anyone from age 18 - 120, unmarried, widowed, or divorced, with or without dependants. The purpose is to come together for fellowship, social activity and spiritual growth.

DUTIES:

1. Regular scheduled fellowship with singles.
2. "Rap" sessions.
3. Social outings.
4. Bible studies and games, contests and seminars.
5. Could elect a governing body to organize and direct the group.
6. Involve the singles with Evangelism and the vision of Vision Christian Church International.

7. See Children's Church for rules of Special speakers.

GOALS: To be active in the community, to be self supporting, to reach out, and to serve the church.

PASTORAL CARE

I. TITLE: Directors

II. PURPOSE: To provide comprehensive pastoral care for all who belong to the church, including new converts, visitors, contacts, and all who seek our ministry.

III. SCOPE.

IV. AREAS OF RESPONSIBILITY:
   A. Supervision.
   B. Co-ordination.
   C. Motivation.
   D. Management.
   E. Development.
   F. Band & Worship Team.
   G. Choirs & Ensembles.
   H. Dance & Drama.
   I. Special Projects.

V. SPECIFIC DUTIES IN EACH AREA:
   A. Supervision - (own initiative)

   1. To guide, assist, and where necessary direct, all the people involved in the various arts, and especially those who lead the various sections (such as the band, drama, ensembles, etc.)

   Standard: your ability to fulfill this task is recognized by the people, so that they turn to you for counsel and guidance.

   2. To give supervision to our arts ministry, but in general to do so by persuasion and example rather than by control or command.

   Standard: your leadership in these areas is established and yielded to cheerfully by the people.

3. Wherever possible to delegate leadership of each section to a gifted person, thereafter to be available primarily as a resource person, counselor, coordinator, facilitator, or in whatever capacity may be necessary to achieve the smooth function and professional performance of each section.

   Standard: successful leaders are established in each section, and they are providing suitable and fruitful music, dance, drama, and other artistic forms of the church.

B. Co-ordination - (own initiative)

To co-ordinate the various arts groups, their programs, their use of the facilities, their human and financial resources; to foresee and take steps to avoid potential conflicts; to achieve harmony between the goals and expressions of each group; to maintain the relative importance and effectiveness of the arts in the church.

Standard: the various groups are all functioning smoothly, and performing regularly, according to the particular nature of each, and conflicts are either avoided or quickly solved.

C. Motivation - (own initiative)

To convey vision and inspiration to those who are already performing in the various arts; to seek out other gifted people in the church and to motivate them to become involved in this ministry.

Standard: the various groups are functioning in the anointing of God, and contributing to the larger vision and growth of the church, while increase is seen in the number of participants and in the quality of their performance.

D. Management - (own initiative)

To guide the overall presentation of the various programs, and their quality; to supervise the use of equipment that belongs to the church; to ensure that the equipment, gowns, etc, required by the various groups are available; to keep the arts department working within its appointed budget.

Standard: the department is running efficiently and economically, and achieving its stated goals of ministering to the church and glorifying Christ through the use of the various arts.

E. Development - (act with approval)

To develop new forms of artistic presentation in the church; new ensembles, dance groups, chorales, and the like; and to develop the facilities and resources available to the various groups and individuals.

Standard: undue repetition of what has been done before is avoided, and there is a steady input of new and creative ways to glorify Christ through the different skills of the performers.

TELEPHONE OUTREACH MINISTRY OF
VISION CHRISTIAN CHURCH INTERNATIONAL

PURPOSE: To extend our welcome from the Pastor to the new visitors and to lovingly guide them to a deeper relationship with Jesus, touching them at their point of need in prayer and agreement, encouraging fellowship with the body of Christ here at Vision.

PROCEDURE:

1. Sign up for a month.
2. All calls are to be made from the church office.
3. All calls are to be logged.
4. No personal calls to be made during this time.
5. All long distance calls are to be logged.
6. Always be encouraging.
7. Be at the church office area at 2:00 p.m. and plan to stay until 4:00 p.m.
8. Current Sunday visitors are to be called first. After that, work backwards.
9. If you are working at a desk, please leave the desk as it was.
10. If a person has questions, refer them to the Word of God.
11. If you do not have an answer for a question, please tell them that

you will find out and call them back. Be sure to ask them what would be a good time for you to call them back.

12. Never promise them that the Pastor will call them back.
13. Have a "Statement of Faith" handy, and refer them to their visitor pack.
14. Encourage them to come back to church and have their questions answered further.
15. Recommend a Home Fellowship in their area. Have your sheet which lists H.F. meetings on it handy. When you finish, place their name card in proper H.F. slot, according to the area in which they reside.
16. Try to meet them personally next Sunday.
17. Never agree to get with them for counseling.

EXAMPLE PHONE CONVERSATION:

"Hello. I'm _____ from Vision Christian Church International. I am calling for Pastor DeKoven. He wants to thank you for coming to the service today. Do you have any prayer needs? Do you know what activities are coming up this week?" Let them know how important they are to the Lord. Hang up on a positive note.

WHY HAVE A TELEPHONE FOLLOW-UP MINISTRY?

A. To extend our welcome from the Pastor to the new visitor.
B. To lovingly guide them to a deeper relationship with Jesus.
C. To touch them at their point of need in prayer and agreement.
D. To encourage fellowship with the Body of Christ here at Vision.
E. To reach out by phone to those who have been born-again through our net team letting them know we care.
F. A phone call will reach a person in a house with acceptance 85% of the time.
G. It is our responsibility to teach new believers. Matthew 28:19&20 says, "Go ye therefore, and teach all nations, baptizing them in the name of the Father, and of the Son and of the Holy Ghost. Teaching them to observe all things whatsoever I have commanded."
H. You are the most important person to them after they have received Christ. You give them the opportunity to know and understand more.

WHAT TYPE OF PEOPLE MAKE THE PHONE MINISTRY EFFECTIVE?

- is it the smart people?
- is it the spiritual people?
- is it the people who know the Bible?
- or is it the people who are faithful?

Is it faithful people who make the phone ministry work - faithfulness is the key to your effectiveness.

Luke 16:10, "He that is faithful in that which is least is faithful also in much."

I Cor. 4:2, "Let a man so account of us, as of the ministers of Christ, and stewards of the mysteries of God. Moreover it is required in stewards, that a man be found faithful."

The phone ministry gives you the experience of dealing with people. As you are faithful in the phone ministry you will begin to see the desires of your heart come to pass.

The key is faithfulness, and all else will be added to you.

The spiritual growth that you are believing God for such as assurance, courage, boldness, firmness, and gentleness will begin to manifest in your life.

Never forget your motivation behind the phone ministry is to "help others."

Phone ministry requires giving and as you are faithful in this area of giving your time, God will entrust greater things into your hands.

Faithfulness guarantees rewards, and you will see results happening in your life.

VISION CHRISTIAN CHURCH INTERNATIONAL - MINISTRY JOB DESCRIPTION

Department: Church Council

Overseer: <u>Senior Pastor</u>

Supervisor: <u>Senior Pastor</u>

Position: Council Member

Leader(s):_____

Goal: To fulfill the Great Commission (Mt. 28:19), and to equip the saints for the work of the ministry. (Eph. 4:11-12)

Objective: To faithfully administer, with God's help and guidance, the responsibilities of your ministry as outlined below.

List of responsibilities:

- The Church Council member will assist the Pastoral Staff through advice and counsel.
- Consider, evaluate and advise on all matters concerning the operation and direction of the local Church, including ministry, business, finance, accounting, etc.
- Be an active member of Vision Christian Fellowship.
- Adhere to Vision Christian Fellowship.
- Pray daily for your Pastors, Regional Leaders, other Council members, and department leaders.
- Attend all meetings of Council, Leaders meetings, promote Church functions.
- Fulfill the criteria listed in I Tim. 3:1-7.
- Function as a liaison between Church members and the Pastor on matters of mutual concern.
- Attend the nearest HG meeting.
- Attend, when possible, HG Regional meetings and Outreaches.
- Recognize and make recommendations for future leadership.
- Council members will be an active leader in a ministry function.

- Set higher goals and objectives for the Departments and review quarterly with Council - work toward attaining these goals.

CHURCH COUNCIL GOALS
1. Evangelism: Give direction and assistance to pastors and other leaders to see:

   a. 100 new Christians.
   b. Plant or support in the planting of 1 new Church and several Bible Colleges as God directs.
   c. Total attendance on Sunday a.m. of 150 by December.

2. Discipleship: Give support to existing New Christians class.

3. Activities:

   a. Develop permanent church facilities.
   b. Put pastors on full compensation.
   c. Update office equipment.

4. Each Council member will be a leader of a department or ministry function.

Pastor Goals
"And my speech and my preaching was not with enticing words of man's wisdom, but in demonstration of the Spirit and of power..." (I Cor. 2:4)

1. To see 50 new Christians added to Vision Christian Fellowship by year's end.
2. To develop ministry teams for Outreach and Church Planting.

VISION CHRISTIAN CHURCH INTERNATIONAL- MINISTRY JOB DESCRIPTION

Department: Education

Overseer: <u>Senior Pastor</u>

Supervisor: <u>Senior Pastor or Associate Minister</u>

Position: Nursery Coordinator

Leader(s):_____

Goal: To fulfill the Great Commission (Mt. 28:19), and to equip the saints for the work of the ministry (Eph. 4:11-12)

Objective: To faithfully administer, with God's help and guidance, the responsibilities of your ministry as outlined below.

List of responsibilities:

1. To insure that children, ages 0-3, are properly cared for during church events. Including: finding supervising personnel, ensuring adequate supplies, cleanliness, etc.
2. Assist in selection of teaching materials.
3. Be an active member of Vision Christian Fellowship.
4. Adhere to V.C.C.I.'s doctrines of faith.
5. Share the vision and goals of the pastors and V.C.C.I.
6. Pray for your nursery children and staff, church, leaders, etc. faithfully.
7. Encourage V.C.C.I. members in your area to attend a home group.
8. Fulfill the criteria listed in I Tim. 3:8-13.
9. Complete required reports and submit to Overseer.
10. Meet periodically with Overseer on matters.
11. Recognize and train potential nursery helpers.
12. Provide counseling support for nursery leaders for problems beyond their expertise.
13. Assist in strengthening nursery leaders through counsel and advice.
14. Set higher goals and objectives for ministry and review quarterly with supervisor - work toward attaining these goals.

VISION CHRISTIAN FELLOWSHIP - MINISTRY JOB DESCRIPTION

Department: Education - Sunday School

Overseer:_____

Supervisor: _____

Position: Superintendent

Leader(s):_____

Goal: To fulfill the Great Commission (Mt. 28:19), and to equip the saints for the work of the ministry (Eph. 4:11-12)

Objective: To faithfully administer, with God's help and guidance, the responsibilities of your ministry as outlined below.

List of responsibilities:

1. To train and teach the children of V.C.C.I. in Biblical concepts.
2. Assist in selection of Sunday school materials.
3. Be an active member of Vision Christian Fellowship.
4. Adhere to V.C.C.I.'s doctrines of faith.
5. Attend all required teacher training sessions, seminars, and assist in teaching.
6. Share the vision and goals of the pastors and V.C.C.I.
7. Be prepared to find or do substitution for sick or absent teachers.
8. Pray for your teachers, church, leaders, etc. faithfully.
9. Coordinate the selection, training, material purchases, supply purchases, and supervise the Sunday School department.
10. Encourage V.C.C.I. members in your area to attend a home group.
11. Fulfill the criteria listed in I Tim. 3:8-13.
12. Complete required reports and submit to Overseer.
13. Meet periodically with Overseer on matters.
14. Recognize and train potential school teachers.
15. Provide counseling support for teachers, for problems beyond their expertise.
16. Assist in strengthening teachers through counsel and advice.
17. Set higher goals and objectives for ministry and review quarterly with supervisor - work toward attaining these goals.

VISION CHRISTIAN FELLOWSHIP - MINISTRY JOB DESCRIPTION

Department: Education - Leadership Training
Overseer:_____

Supervisor: _____

Position: Training Supervisor

Leader(s):_____

Goal: To fulfill the Great Commission (Mt. 28:19), and to equip the saints for the work of the ministry (Eph. 4:11-12)

Objective: To faithfully administer, with God's help and guidance, the responsibilities of your ministry as outlined below.

List of responsibilities:

1. To develop and implement a comprehensive adult (16+) leadership program.
2. Select all teaching materials.
3. Be an active member of Vision Christian Fellowship.
4. Adhere to V.C.C.I.'s doctrines of faith.
5. Attend all required teacher training sessions, seminars, etc.
6. Share the vision and goals of the pastors and V.C.C.I.
7. Pray for your church, leaders, etc. faithfully.
8. Encourage V.C.C.I. members in your area to attend a home group.
9. Fulfill the criteria listed in I Tim. 3:8-13.
10. Complete required reports and submit to Overseer.
11. Meet periodically with Overseer on matters.
12. Recognize and train potential teachers/leaders.
13. Provide counseling support for teachers/leaders, for problems beyond their expertise.
14. Assist in strengthening teachers/leaders through counsel and advice.
15. Set higher goals and objectives for ministry and review quarterly with supervisor - work toward attaining these goals.

EDUCATION LEADERSHIP GOALS
"Train up a child in the way he should go: and when he is old, he will not depart from it." (Prov. 22:6)

"And he gave some, apostles; and some, prophets; and some, evangelists; and some, pastors and teachers; For the perfecting of the saints, for the work of the ministry, for the edifying of the body of Christ..." (Eph. 4:11-12)

1. We will complete development of a comprehensive family oriented educational program for leadership training.
2. Primary classes will be conducted Tues. evening, 7:00 - 9:00 with periodic seminars in *Ramona Institute for Christian Leadership. They will cover, but not be limited to:

   a. New Christians
   b. Characters Change
   c. Parent/Child Relations
   d. Marriage and Family
   e. Seniors/Singles
   f. Bible College Classes
   g. Counseling and Church Needs

* Affiliated with Vision International College & University.

APPENDICES

APPENDIX 1
APPLICATION FOR MINISTRY

VISION CHRISTIAN CHURCH INTERNATIONAL
1115 D Street
RAMONA, CA. 92065
PERSONAL RECOMMENDATION
TO THE APPLICANT (Please type or Print)

APPLICANT'S
NAME_____
       LAST   FIRST   MIDDLE
ADDRESS:_____
      STREET   CITY   ZIP
TELEPHONE NUMBER (_____)_____

I understand that this confidential statement is being submitted directly to the office of Vision Christian Church International with the understanding that its contents will not be shared with me. I hereby waive my right to see the confidential statement submitted on this form. (This form is to be mailed directly to Vision by the individual completing the recommendation.)

_____
Signature

_____
Date
****

TO THE INDIVIDUAL
Thank you for your assistance in filling out this recommendation. Serious consideration will be given to your comments; therefore, we ask that you complete the form carefully. It should be returned directly to: Vision Christian Fellowship, 1115 D Street, Ramona, Ca. 92065. Since we request a candid evaluation, we will hold your comments in strictest confidence.

1. How long have you known the applicant?

2. How well do you know him/her? (check one)
_____ By name/sight
_____ Casually; few personal contacts
_____ Fairly well; numerous personal contacts
_____ Very Close; pastoral relationship

3. Please indicate applicant's level of involvement in church activities. (check one)
_____ Attends irregularly - shows little interest
_____ Seldom participates although attends regularly
_____ Cooperative; usually willing to help
_____ Enthusiastic; deeply involved

4. What do you consider the applicant's strong points (include positive personal traits)?

_____
_____
_____

5. What do you consider the applicant's weak points (include negative personal traits)?

_____
_____

6. How do you rate this person in the following areas:

Excellent/Above Average/Below Average/No chance to observe

Leadership _____
Responsibility_____
Christian Commitment_____
Initiative_____
Cooperativeness_____
Personal Appearance_____
Moral Character_____
Health _____
Social Adaptability_____
Integrity and Honesty_____
Emotional Stability_____

7. Do you believe the applicant is called into the full-time ministry?

_____

_____

8. Please share with us any information you may have about the applicant that would help in our evaluation. This information could cover recent experience or incidents in the applicant's life or even a general personality appraisal.

_____

_____

_____

_____

9. Please check the terms which best describe the applicant's attitude toward the church and its activities.

_____Warmhearted	_____Enthusiastic	_____Loving
_____Sympathetic	_____Respectful	_____Tolerant
_____Passive	_____Contemptuous	_____Critical

_____

Signature

_____

Name

_____

Street

_____

City   Zip

_____

Area code   Phone number

APPENDIX 2

VISION CHRISTIAN CHURCH INTERNATIONAL APPLICATION FOR MEMBERSHIP

To the Pastor and Church Council:

Having completed the required course of study, and being in full agreement with the principles embodied in the Charter of Vision Christian Church International, and believing that this is the will of God, I respectfully submit to you this application for membership in the church.
I have accepted Jesus Christ as my personal Savior and Lord (Rom. 10:8-11).

I have been baptized in water, by full immersion, subsequent to my confession of faith in Christ (Mt. 28:19-20; Acts 2:38-39).

I agree to submit to the oversight of the church in matters of doctrine, Christian conduct, and the disciplinary authority of the church (Eph. 5:20; Heb. 13:17; I Thess. 5:12,13).

I agree not to pursue legal action or to sue the pastors, counselors, directors or any other member of the church staff, whether directly or indirectly, in connection with the performance of their official and scriptural duties (I Cor. 6:1-8).

I agree to be faithful and generous in supporting the church in tithes and offerings, as the Lord prospers me (I Cor. 16:2; II Cor. 9:6-7; Heb. 13:16).

I do not hold current membership in any other church.

I would like to transfer my membership from _____
church located at _____.

Signed:_____
Date:_____

(Please complete also the details requested on this page.)

PERSONAL INFORMATION
(Please print legibly)
LAST NAME:_____
FIRST NAME:_____
ADDRESS:_____
_____ZIP_____
TELEPHONE:_____
DATE OF BIRTH:_____

The year (if known) of your:
Conversion:_____
Water Baptism:_____
Holy Spirit Baptism:_____
Are you single_____ married_____ widowed_____
divorced/separated_____

If married, the full name of your spouse:

_____

The full name and ages of minor children:

_____
_____
_____
_____

Do you have any gifts or skills that could be employed in the service of the church?

_____
_____
_____

Is there some office or function in the church that you would like an opportunity to fulfill?

_____
_____
_____

VISION CHRISTIAN FELLOWSHIP CHARTER QUESTIONNAIRE

If you desire to become a member of this local church, the following Questionnaire must first be completed, and then returned to the local church, along with your application for membership.

Your full name (please print):

_____

For each of the following questions select and correctly answer and then place a cross (X) in the appropriate square on your answer sheet. You may, of course, use your copy of the Charter to help you find the correct answers. Feel free, also, to work with a friend, and to discuss the questions together. The purpose of this Questionnaire is simply to assure the Church Council that you are familiar with the doctrines and practices of the church.

1. Have you read through the Charter?
   a. Yes
   b. No

2. Which of these Biblical texts best expresses the mission of this church?
   a. John 3:16
   b. Hebrews 2:3-4
   c. Romans 15:18-19

3. Our doctrinal statement is based upon the idea that...
   a. Those great Biblical doctrines that are held by all of the major branches of the church should be generally accepted.
   b. The Bible is not the only source of sound doctrine and practice.
   c. From the beginning of their history the older denominations have erred in their major doctrines.

4. Which of the following is needed to complete this statement from the Charter? "Eternal life and inheritance of the kingdom of God depend upon coming into spiritual union with Christ, and upon...
   a. following Him through the waters of baptism."

    b. yielding to the Lordship of Christ."

    c. maintaining close fellowship with His church."

5. The healing covenant described in James 5:13-16...
    a. does not preclude the use of medical science.
    b. suggests that we should not call upon a physician.
    c. is not a paradigm for the church today.

6. We view the church as being primarily...
    a. a working community.
    b. a witnessing community.
    c. a worshipping community.

7. Concerning God's promise of financial and material prosperity:
    a. it was part of the old covenant, but is not part of the new.
    b. it does not depend solely upon faith, for certain conditions are attached to it.
    c. it is crass to take it literally, for it must be understood spiritually or figuratively.

8. "Each Christian must always retain the right to dissent from any authority save that of conscience." That statement...
    a. reflects what is written in the Charter.
    b. opposes what is written in the Charter.
    c. has nothing to do with the Charter.

9. According to the Charter...
    a. infant baptism and believer's baptism are equally valid.
    b. membership is available only to those who have been baptized in our church.
    c. baptism, if properly administered and received, will convey divine grace to the recipient.

10. Which of the following did Christ specifically command his followers do corporately?
    a. Fast every week.
    b. Celebrate Communion.
    c. Bring their tithes to church.

11. "Full maturity in Christ is hardly attainable without regular participation at the Lord's Table." That sentence...
    a. reflects what is written in the Charter.
    b. opposes what is written in the Charter.
    c. has nothing to do with the Charter.

12. Under the Lordship of Christ, ultimate authority in the local church is vested in the...
    a. the senior pastor.
    b. the presbytery.
    c. the members' meeting.

13. The authority of the presbytery is...
    a. absolute.
    b. advisory.
    c. ancillary.

14. The authority of the people is based upon...
    a. The democratic rights of the majority.
    b. the maturity of the corporate body.
    c. the priesthood each believer has in Christ.

15. "There may be times in the life of the church when a democratic vote will be the best way to discover the will of God." Which of the following is a proper response to that statement?
    a. It is true, because the Lord is free to bypass "official" channels whenever He pleases, and if He chooses, to speak to the church through its humblest member.
    b. It is false, because the good order of the kingdom requires that God should always express His will through those who are His anointed under-shepherds.
    c. When such a democratic vote is taken it must be yielded to by the pastors and by the church council, for it is binding upon the whole church.

16. Which of the following is given in the Charter as a purpose for the annual member's meeting?
    a. To elect the church council.
    b. To allow the people opportunity for expression.
    c. To determine the doctrines of the church.

17. Attendance at our communion service is...
    a. expected of all members, but is not mandatory.
    b. obligatory in order to retain membership.
    c. required at least 45 times per annum.

18. Which of the following is not given in the Charter as one of the "Conditions for Membership"?
    a. Weekly payment of at least a tithe of your income.
    b. You may not hold membership in any other church.
    c. You must accept the rules and principles embodied in the Charter.

19. New members are brought into the church...
    a. by a majority of the existing membership.
    b. after paying tithes for at least one month.
    c. by the laying-on of hands in an open meeting.

20. Which of the following is not a valid ground for removal from the membership of the church?
    a. Failure to be baptized in the Holy Spirit and to speak in tongues.
    b. Absence from the regular services for a period of three consecutive months.
    c. Unscriptural conduct, such as divisiveness, violence, drunkenness, and the like.

21. A person who has been removed from the membership of the church...
    a. must wait three years before re-applying for membership.
    b. may be restored to fellowship and membership at any time.
    c. may be restored to membership after paying a fine or some other penalty.

22. Which of the following is not one of the methods of discipline employed by this church?
    a. Exclusion from participation in the Communion.
    b. Suspension of fellowship with the other members of the church.
    c. Publication of the person's offence in the church bulletin.

23. How many classes of credentials is this church authorized to issue?
    a. One.
    b. Two.
    c. Three.

24. The five ministry-gifts described in Ephesians are..
    a. Apostles, prophets, teachers, bishops, deacons.
    b. Bishops, deacons, elders, presbyters, pastors.
    c. Apostles, prophets, evangelists, pastors, teachers.

CHARTER QUESTIONNAIRE ANSWER SHEET

1) _____
2) _____
3) _____
4) _____
5) _____
6) _____
7) _____
8) _____
9) _____
10) _____
11) _____
12) _____

13) _____
14) _____
15) _____
16) _____
17) _____
18) _____
19) _____
20) _____
21) _____
22) _____
23) _____
24) _____

APPENDIX 3

Letter of Welcome

Welcome to Vision International Ministries. As a member of our board and/or staff, you are vital to the success of our mission - to equip leaders for effective ministry.

It is imperative that you familiarize yourself with all aspects of this manual. It was designed to inform, assist and strengthen each other in our mutual goal, and to insure that we all "sing the same song."

If you have any questions regarding any policy or procedure found in this manuscript, please discuss it thoroughly with your supervisor. All the policies are subject to periodic review, and we appreciate your prayerful input.

Again, welcome aboard. We are so glad you are a part of this dynamic ministry - God Bless.

Dr. Stan E. DeKoven, Ph.D.
President

Introduction

A part of administration of a healthy local church or other ministry is promotion through policies. By promotion, I mean the process of informing adherents and potential adherents of the vision, purposes, programs, and possibilities of your work for God. With good, honest and well presented promotion (Write the vision; make it plain, that others will proclaim it, Hab. 2:1-3), your members will know what they are a part of and who they relate to and will have ammunition for inviting others to be a part.

To follow are some ideas concepts that can be used to promote a vision. Of course, you are only limited by your imagination and budget. It is advised that this or similar material be put into a booklet or brochure form for all members' usage, and to provide to those interested in membership.

I. Purpose

It is the policy of Vision International Ministries to develop and maintain a Policy and Procedures Manual intended to serve as a primary medium of communications to inform supervisory personnel of the following:

A. Approved personnel and operating policies and procedures;
B. Employee benefit plans in effect;
C. Responsibilities and authorization within the organization;
D. Organization structure.

II. Manual Objectives

The objectives of the Policy and Procedures Manual are as follows:

A. To promote uniform understanding and application of Church/Ministry policy.
B. To identify responsibility and authority for the administration of Church/Ministry policies and procedures.
C. To standardize the handling of recurring personnel administration matters.
D. To provide guidance for personnel administration matters that resist standardization.

E. To provide a working guide for use in counseling employees and in training newly appointed supervisory personnel.

F. To provide an established point of reference for use in auditing and determining the need for improving existing policies and practices.

This Policy & Procedures Manual and all its policies and procedures inclusive were approved by the Board of Directors on Dec. 18, 1994.

INTRODUCTION

This Policies and Procedures Manual has been prepared for the purpose of providing general information and guidelines concerning the policies, practices, and procedures for conducting the official business of Vision Christian Church/Ministry International, Inc, dba Vision International College and University and Vision International Network, dba Vision Publishing, Walk in Wisdom Ministries, and the Vision Family Care Center. During the first day of employment, a copy of the manual will be issued to each new employee, who is instructed to read it carefully and become thoroughly familiar with its contents.

The manual has been prepared in the hope that it will give each employee a better understanding of the organizational structure of Vision, the duties and responsibilities of its officers and employees, and its methods of work as the means of achieving its mission.

Throughout this handbook, VCCI/VCN shall be referred to as Vision.

1. Questions Regarding the Manual:

If you have any questions concerning anything contained in the manual, you are instructed to bring the matter to the attention of the head of your Office or Department, after you have carefully searched through the manual for the answer.

2. Revisions and Changes:

Revisions and changes may be made in the manual at any time, without notice, at the sole discretion of the President and Human Resource Director. Suggestions for additions or corrections are welcomed and should be submitted to the Human Resource Director for consideration.

As changes and revisions are approved and become effective, they shall be issued to each Office and Department. All Offices and Departments are directed to add to their manual all new materials as soon as it is available.

3. Manual is Property of the Ministry:

This manual is not a contract of employment. It shall remain the property of the ministry. You are instructed to deliver your copy of the manual to the Human Resource Director on the last day of your employment with the ministry.

EMPLOYEE ACKNOWLEDGMENT FORM

The employee handbook describes important information about Vision and I understand that I should consult the Administrator regarding any questions not answered in the handbook. I have entered into my employment relationship with the Church/Ministry voluntarily and acknowledge that there is no specified length of employment, unless stated in a contract between the Church/Ministry and myself. Accordingly, either the Church/Ministry or I can terminate the relationship at will, with or without cause, at any time, so long as there is no violation of applicable federal or state law.

Since the information, policies, and benefits described here are necessarily subject to change, I acknowledge that revisions to the handbook may occur, except to the Church/Ministry's policy of employment-at-will. All such changes will be communicated through official notices, and I understand that revised information may supersede, modify, or eliminate existing policies. Only the Church/Ministry Board has the ability to adopt any revisions to the policies in this handbook.

Furthermore, I acknowledge that this handbook is neither a contract of employment nor a legal document. I have received the handbook, and I understand that it is my responsibility to read and comply with the policies contained in this handbook and any revisions made to it.

Also, I understand that I am being employed by a Church/Ministry, and that Church/Ministries are exempt from unemployment insurance regulations. Therefore, I may not be eligible to receive unemployment benefits for the period I am employed by the Church/Ministry.

Employee's Signature   Date

Employee's Name (Typed or Printed)

(After the acknowledgement has been signed by the employee, make one copy of the form, file the original signed form in the employee's personnel file, and give the copy to the employee for his or her manual.)

VISION OF VISION

As with every great endeavor, whether in the natural world or God's spiritual Kingdom, there are many circumstances, events, conflicts and influences which determine the effectiveness of the endeavor.

Historically, triumphs came within the context of history, where generally common men and women were thrust to the forefront, and rose to the challenge at hand. Without the evil Pharaoh, would a Moses have been required? Without Saul's turning away from God, David's triumph would not have been needed. Without the captivity, Daniel and the three Hebrew children may not have had such monumental influence, and Ezra and Nehemiah would not have had walls to rebuild and revival fires to flame. Even in modem history, without the evil empire of Hitler, would Roosevelt, DeGaulle and Churchill, let alone Bradley, Eisenhower and Patton, have become admirable heroes in spite of their clear human weakness.

All of history, and every truly significant ministry, has come into being as with Esther, "for such a time as this." Of course, all of the human vessels that God has used throughout history have been imperfect, yet God in His mercy and grace chooses whomever He will to fulfill His purpose. He has always done things according to the counsel of His own will, and always shall.

Throughout the world, both in the world and in the church, there is a cry for leadership. A deep yearning exists for men and women of moral integrity and a sincere desire to help God's chosen people who will arise with a fresh vision for the future. Unsatisfied with the status quo, men and women are anxiously awaiting for a true leader who can bring them a sense of meaning, purpose and hope. For such a time as this is the call for visionary leaders, who will dedicate themselves to the task of changing the world.

Jesus Christ came into the world during a similar time. The Roman Government, with their ideology and idolatry, was dominating the known world. God's chosen people were languishing in Palestine, oppressed and powerless. Their glorious past was all but forgotten under the oppressive hand of the Romans.

One would think the Hebrews would be somewhat used to their lot. Throughout their history, as with the history of the New Testament Church, their fate seemed to rise and fall in direct proportion to the obedience and vision (or lack thereof) of their leaders. When the leaders obeyed the Word of the Lord and followed righteousness, all was well. Ultimately, prosperity became their portion. When they walked in disobedience and rebellion, captivity, bondage and a lack of power or fulfillment became their lot.

As it has been said, there is nothing new under the sun. As we also observe in history, God is gracious and plenteous in mercy. God has never forgotten this covenant to the people of Abraham, Isaac, and Jacob, or those grafted into the covenant by the blood of His precious Son Jesus. God has always provided a Moses, Gideon, Deborah, David, Hezekiah, Nehemiah, Ezra, Jesus, Luther or Wesley. Modem history also provides for us ample examples of faithful men and women, filled with the power of God, who have provided a message and model of hope to each subsequent generation.

As we observe the signs of our times, it becomes only too apparent that we are in need for a deliverer, a visionary leader who can show Christ's Church the direction that it desperately needs.

WHERE TO LOOK, WHOM TO SEEK

Some would look outside of the church for such leadership. Many would look to political power, or attempt to lead through building a financial empire, but ultimately, God will raise up leaders in this generation who have His heart, and His vision, and will in an uncompromising fashion lead the people of God as we prepare for the coming of the Lord.

Other Christians long for a great spiritual leader. We should remember and give honor to those who have provided a foundation for us to build upon. However, in this final (we hope) outpouring of God's Holy Spirit, it will not be one or a few but thousands and tens of thousands of common men and women who will know their God, display strength and take action (Daniel 11:32 NAS). It is the time for the Joshua generation to emerge and take their place in the harvest field, which is the Kingdom of God.

THE EVERLASTING VISION

Jesus told His disciples to make disciples of all nations. This would occur through identification (salvation/baptism) with Christ and through teaching them (Matt. 28:18-20). The primary vision of Vision is to provide the resources necessary to effectively teach, equip, and restore those who through identification with the death, burial and resurrection of Christ are destined for service in God's Kingdom. Every believer in every nation must go beyond simple (yet profound) identification to full discipleship, maturity and wholeness in Christ, and thus compassionately live out their life in humble submission to Christ and His Word.

The vision, given to us by the Lord through His progressive revelation includes the following:

THE THREE LEGS

First, the local church is the central place of all of God's purposes. The church was not an afterthought of God, but has been in His vision from the beginning. The church today is the laboratory for the equipping/restoring of God's people. It is thus the central leg of God's Holy tripod. Of course, for a tripod (three-threaded cord, etc.) to be strong, it must have its other legs. The second leg being the Healing or Restoration Center. The church, like a hospital, must be prepared to repair and rebuild the broken lives who enter her.

When men and women are saved out of darkness they bring their deeds of darkness, often hidden in their hearts, into the church. The results of the work of the devil in the lives of people, the impact of a sin-tainted environment causes damage to the soul and body that needs loving care and appropriate medicine. This can include counseling, practical guidance, group support, and loving biblical confrontation over time to see results that are lasting. The third leg, the mirror of leg two, is that of equipping or training. Every church should be a worship center, every church should be a healing center and every church should be a training center, where believers can be systematically trained according to biblical pattern (see Acts 2:42; 11:19-26; 19:8-11). This training or education must be systematic, anointed, academic, and filled with life.

The Vision of Vision is to provide to the Body of Christ assistance, support, encouragement and resources to strengthen all three legs, and thus facilitate the preparation of the Bride of Christ for the Bridegroom (Rev. 19:7)

THE SERVICES OF VISION

As a comprehensive ministry, Vision International Ministries provides the following services on a National/International basis:

I. **Vision Christian Church International Educational Network**
    a. **Vision International University**, External Study (home study) with short term residence offering Bachelors completion through Doctoral degrees, this program has been designed to eventually achieve full institutional approval.
    b. **Vision International University - College of Biblical Studies and Theology** - colleges offering satellite campuses in local churches with faculty mentors.
    c. **Leadership in Vision Conferences**, annual conferences and seminars, in cooperation with several outstanding ministries, Assembly of God International Fellowship, A.L. Gill Ministries, Good Shepherd Ministries, Barnabas Ministries, Harvest International Ministries, Dr. Randy Gurley, in the US and Canada and around the world, providing residency opportunity for VIU students and encouragement/training for leaders where Bible Colleges have been established.
    d. **Vision International Network of Ministers and Ministries** - Local Fellowship and International Fellowship of Churches and Ministers.

II. **Vision Christian Ministries, Inc. Counseling and Guidance Services**

    a. **Family Care Network** provides for training and assistance in establishing counseling ministries in local churches.
    b. **American Society for Christian Therapists** provides for Certification and support for qualified Christian Therapists around the world.

c. **Personal Counseling** for leaders suffering from burnout, personal crisis or family problems on a confidential professional basis.
d. **Church Assistance** in "Setting the House in Order" with administrative and personal consulting.

III. Literature and Media

a. **Vision Publishing** provides for high quality courses, books, booklets, manuals, video tapes and cassettes to provide for continuing education, and in support of the educational goals of Vision.

PHILOSOPHY OF VISION INTERNATIONAL

1. The Doctrinal Statement
The doctrinal statement, which is also available in the catalog, is as follows:

Doctrines

This is not intended to be a comprehensive statement of faith (as seen in our Articles of Incorporation), but rather a guide to the doctrinal boundaries within which the college functions. Those who share our spiritual identity will be generally familiar with the following terms, and will be able to fill in what is lacking. However, if you desire clarification of any point, do not hesitate to inquire. We will be pleased to give you details of our stance upon any doctrinal position. We believe:

- That there is only one God, who has revealed Himself as the Father, the Son, and the Holy Spirit.

- In the absolute Lordship and deity of Christ, including His pre-existence, His virgin birth, His sinless life, His atoning death, His bodily resurrection, and His eventual return to the earth in glory and power to establish His eternal kingdom.

- That nothing can replace the importance of the local church in the program of God.

- That the great task of the Church is worldwide evangelism.

- That entrance into the church is through the "new birth" which is brought about by genuine repentance of sin, confession of faith in Christ as the only Savior, and surrender to Him as Lord.

- That membership in the Church is signified by joyful participation in its worship, fellowship, sacraments, witness, and by acceptance of its discipline.

- That the ministry of the Holy Spirit is an essential component of effective ministry.

- Christian life and witness.

- That the church cannot fulfill its mission apart from the five ascension gift ministries that Christ has sent into the world: apostles, prophets, evangelists, pastors and teachers. We accept that it is part of our responsibility to recognize those people and to assist in equipping them to fulfill their ministry.

- That Christ purchased healing for every believer at Calvary, and this healing can and should be appropriated by faith.

- In the reality of Satan, and the kingdom of darkness over which he reigns. We believe also in the absolute triumph of Christ over the devil and all his works.

- That victorious Christian life is built upon a proper understanding and exercise of the spiritual authority conveyed to the believer by the gift of righteousness.

- In the resurrection of the dead at Christ's return, in the certainty of God's judgment, and in the inescapable result of that judgment foretold in the Scriptures for the just and for the unjust.

Development of the Statement of Philosophy

The institutional philosophy is stated in our catalog on pages 8-9.

The philosophy was developed by the Academic Dean in consultation with the President in 1991. This was then presented to the Executive Board and the Board of Regents for their approval. This was approved on September 12, 1993.

<u>Adherence to the Doctrinal Statement</u>

All faculty and students are required to sign the statement, thereby affirming their agreement.

Approved September 12, 1993, Board of Regents.

MISSION STATEMENT

The comprehensive purpose of Vision International is to provide a high quality Christian education for the individual development of each student for the responsibilities of Christian life as well as for leadership and service in the various Christian ministries.

The Vision International University mission is to provide high quality education to the whole person; body, mind, and spirit - for Christian ministry at the college level for responsible Christian living, leadership, and service. Programmed study in Biblical and theological education along with general and professional education is for the purpose of cultivating success in the following ministries: (1) Theology and Bible studies, (2) Christian Counseling, (3) Christian Education, (4) Christian Business Management.

<u>THE VISION</u>

During the 70's and 80's, the Church of Jesus Christ has gone through many transitions. Traditional religion is no longer effective. We need the outpouring of God's Spirit. As we move toward the year 2006, there is an expectation of World revival. God is raising up ministries which have, at their core, a bond-slave mentality, with a desire to win the world to Jesus Christ in this generation. In order to do this, a radical change in strategy must occur. Indigenous works must be raised up and lay leadership mobilized. Leaders must be encouraged, materials developed for proper teaching, and support for God's wounded warriors provided. We believe that God has placed a tool in our hands and has given birth to a vision in our hearts to raise up and support leaders who are on fire for God, and who will bring revival to the nations.

THE PURPOSE

Our purpose can be best described in our motto "equipping the church to reach the world." We are actively involved in the training, restoring and releasing of pastors, teachers, counselors, and lay leaders into effective and response Christian Service. Our focus is the inner city, indigenous missions, and evangelistic fields. In all of our training material, we desire to instill in the student an expectancy of God's outpouring, a prophetic call to preparing spiritually. Evangelistically, we desire to reach our world and to disciple men and women into "the fullness of the stature of Christ." To this purpose we have gladly sold ourselves, faithfully believing that God will perform that which He has begun.

THE PLAN

I wish I could say that the plan for the ministry was brilliantly devised by its principal parties. The truth is, God revealed a plan, and we are doing our best to fulfill it. Essentially, the plan has 3 aspects, and each one of these different components comes under the responsibility of at least one of our two affiliate corporations. The three components are as follows:

- Training/Education - We see our function as an educational/discipleship ministry which includes developing books and manuals, adult education courses, seminar workshops, radio/TV, tapes/video, to effectively train and educate men and women for the work of Christ.

- Restoration Counseling - The Body of Christ needs healing and restoration. Through the counseling and rehabilitation ministries we are helping hundreds reach wholeness in Christ.

- Consulting/Planting - More than teaching, we are assisting local churches and national ministries to be more effective in the counseling, training, rehabilitation, church planting, and Bible Institute development endeavors.

PERSONNEL POLICIES AND PROCEDURES

NATURE OF EMPLOYMENT

Employment with Vision is voluntarily entered into, and the employee is free to resign at will at any time, with or without cause. Similarly, the Church may terminate the employment relationship at will at any time, with or without notice or cause, so long as there is no violation of applicable federal or state law.

Policies set forth in this handbook are not intended to create a contract, nor are they to be construed to constitute contractual obligations of any kind or a contract of employment between Vision and any of its employees. The provisions of the handbook have been developed at the discretion of the Church Board and, except for its policy of employment-at-will, may be amended or canceled at any time, at the Church's sole discretion.

These provisions supersede all existing policies and practices and may not be amended or added to without the express written approval of the Board of Directors.

EMPLOYEE RELATIONS

Vision believes that the work conditions, wages, and benefits it offers to its employees are competitive with those offered by other churches in this area and size. If employees have concerns about work conditions or compensation, they are strongly encouraged to voice these concerns openly and directly to the Administrator.

Our experience has shown that when employees deal openly and directly with supervisors, the work environment can be excellent, communications can be clear, and attitudes can be positive. We believe that amply demonstrates its commitment to employees by responding effectively to employee concerns.

EQUAL EMPLOYMENT OPPORTUNITY

In order to provide equal employment and advancement opportunities to all individuals, employment decisions at Vision will be based on merit, qualifications, and abilities. The Church does not discriminate in employment opportunities or practices on the basis of race, color, sex, national origin, age, disability, or any other characteristic protected by law as it applies to churches.

The Equal Pay Act of 1963 protects men and women who perform substantially equal work under similar working conditions in the same establishment from sex-based wage discrimination. The law prohibits employers from reducing the wages of either sex to comply with the law.

Title VII of the Civil Rights Act of 1964 applies to employers with 15 or more employees. The Act prohibits employment discrimination based on race, color, sex, or national origin. Under Title VII, it is illegal to discriminate in: hiring and firing; compensation; assignment or classification of employees; transfer, promotion, layoff or recall; job advertisements; recruitment; testing; use of company facilities; training and apprenticeship programs; fringe benefits; pay, retirement plans and disability leave; or other terms and conditions of employment. Pregnancy, childbirth and related medical conditions must be treated the same as any other non-pregnancy-related illness or disability.

The Age Discrimination in Employment Act of 1967 protects employees 40 years of age or older in hiring, discharge, pay, promotions and other terms or conditions of employment. The law applies to employers with 20 or more employees.

The Americans with Disabilities Act (ADA) became effective July 26, 1992, for all organizations with 25 or more employees, and on July 26, 1994, for all organizations with 15 or more employees.

The ADA does not allow discrimination against individuals with physical or mental impairment. Examples of these disabilities are: blind, hearing impaired, confined to a wheelchair, AIDS, cancer, heart disease, diabetes, mental retardation, or learning disabilities.

The Church will make reasonable accommodations for qualified individuals with known disabilities unless doing so would result in an undue hardship. This policy governs all aspects of employment, including selection, job assignment, compensation, discipline, termination, and access to benefits and training.

Any employees with questions or concerns about any type of discrimination in the workplace are encouraged to bring these issues to the attention of their immediate supervisor or the Administrator. Employees can raise concerns and make reports without fear of reprisal. Anyone found to be engaging in any type of unlawful discrimination will be subject to disciplinary action, up to and including termination of employment.

INTERVIEWING

Since several laws now regulate the questions an employer may ask when considering an applicant for employment, an interview form has been designed to assist in compliance. The questions have been phrased in a way to get the answers an employer needs from an applicant and still stay within the various restrictions placed by the laws in effect.

The only questions that should be asked are those that give information about how well an applicant can perform a job. Questions that reflect negatively on age, race, national origin, sex or disability are generally unnecessary and do not reveal relevant information about job performance.

Since the employer is a Church, it is permissible to ask the applicant if he or she is a Christian. The Church may not require the applicant to be a member of their Church or even their specific religion, except ministerial staff. It has been agreed by the government agencies, however, that Church employees work so closely with church members that they need a general understanding of the religious beliefs of their employer. This has resulted in the opinion that a Buddhist or Muslim, for instance, might have difficulty performing the duties required by a Christian employer.

Some of the questions an interviewer may not ask are:

1. Any questions regarding an applicant's marital status or concerning the number or age of children, pregnancy, child bearing or birth control.

2. Questions to determine whether or not the applicant has children, and if so, the arrangements made for day care.
3. Whether or not the applicant's spouse objects to the applicant traveling.
4. Any type of questions regarding an applicant, applicant's parents or spouse concerning their birthplace, national origin, whether they are native-born or naturalized citizens or the complexion or color of their skin, eyes and hair.
5. Questions to determine if the applicant is a citizen of this country.
6. Inquiries to determine how the applicant learned to speak a foreign language.
7. Asking an applicant for her maiden name.
8. Any question regarding age, birth-date, dates of attendance of a particular school.
9. Asking when the applicant graduated from high school.
10. Questions regarding an applicant's disability, general health, height, weight, treatments for drug addiction or alcoholism, or receipt of workers compensation.
11. Asking the applicant about the nature or severity of his or her disability.
12. Questions regarding an arrest without a conviction or concerning refusal or cancellation of bonding.
13. Questions regarding type of discharge from military service.
14. Questions concerning an applicant's bankruptcy or garnishment.
15. Asking if the applicant owns a car.
16. Questions on whether the applicant owns or rents his or her home.

The first section of the interview form is designed to provide more revealing information about a job candidate. In an ideal interview, the applicant should be talking about 75% of the time to reveal as much as possible about the person.

The second section of the interview form deals with permissible questions of a more personal nature that can be asked during an interview.

The interviewer may wish to add or delete certain questions depending on the job for which the applicant is applying. These questions should be specific to the duties of the position. If the decision is made to add questions, be certain none of the rules shown in the preceding paragraphs are broken.

A good interviewer takes few notes during the interview. Try to limit note-taking to just job-specific issues. After the interview is over, you may make additional notes regarding the applicant.

Even though an applicant is not hired, the interviewer should keep the application, any interview notes, and a summary of the reasons the applicant was not hired for several months. These items provide protection for the organization in the event the applicant files a complaint with a government agency charging some form of discrimination.

EMPLOYMENT CATEGORIES

It is the intent of Vision to clarify the definitions of employment classifications so that employees understand their employment status and benefits eligibility. These classifications do not guarantee employment for any specified period of time. Accordingly, the right to terminate the employment relationship at will at any time is retained by both the employee and the Church.

REGULAR FULL-TIME employees are those who are not in a temporary, introductory or casual status and who are regularly scheduled to work the Church's full-time schedule. Generally, they are eligible for the Church's benefit package, subject to the terms, conditions, and limitations of each benefit program.

PART-TIME employees are those who are not assigned to a temporary or introductory status and who are regularly scheduled to work less than 24 hours per week. While they do receive all legally mandated benefits (such as workers' compensation insurance), they are ineligible for all of the Church's other benefit programs.

INTRODUCTORY employees are those whose performance is being evaluated to determine whether further employment in a specific position or with the Church is appropriate. While introductory employees receive all legally mandated benefits (such as workers' compensation insurance), they are ineligible for all of the Church's other benefit programs.

Employees who satisfactorily complete the introductory period will be notified of their new employment classification.

TEMPORARY employees are those who are hired as interim replacements, to temporarily supplement the work force, or to assist in the completion of a specific project. Employment assignments in this category are of a limited duration. Employment beyond any initially stated period does not in any way imply a change in employment status. Temporary employees retain that status unless and until notified of a change. While temporary employees receive all legally mandated benefits (such as workers' compensation insurance), they are ineligible for all of the Church's other benefit programs.

CASUAL employees are those who have established an employment relationship with the Church but who are assigned to work on an intermittent and/or unpredictable basis. While they receive all legally mandated benefits (such as workers' compensation insurance), they are ineligible for all of the Church's other benefit programs.

NOTE ON SOCIAL SECURITY AND MEDICARE

The Church has filed a Form 8274 with the Internal Revenue Service. This exempts the Church from paying Social Security and Medicare taxes on behalf of its employees. Instead, employees are subject to the Self-Employment Compensation Act (SECA).

All employees are responsible for paying 15.3% for coverage under the Act. Employees may request the Church deduct the additional tax in the form of Federal Income Tax from their pay. Otherwise, employees are responsible for paying the tax directly to the Internal Revenue Service.

Employees are required to file a Schedule SE with their Federal Income Tax Form 1040 each year to calculate and report Self-Employment Tax due on their earnings.

In addition to the previous categories, each employee will belong to one other employment category:

Each employee is designated as either NONEXEMPT or EXEMPT from federal and state wage and hour laws. NONEXEMPT employees are entitled to minimum wage and overtime pay under the specific provisions of federal and state laws. EXEMPT employees are excluded from specific provisions of federal and state wage and hour laws. An employee's EXEMPT or NONEXEMPT classification may be changed only upon written notification by the Board.

EXEMPT employees are those who meet specific criteria which exempts them from minimum wage and/or overtime law coverage. These include executives, administrative staff, and professionals.

Paying an employee a set salary does not automatically make the employee exempt. An employee may be paid a set salary and still not qualify for exemption from minimum wage and overtime provisions. A nonexempt employee, who is paid a salary, must be paid extra for working more than 40 hours in a workweek.

The following paragraphs define the conditions for qualifications in each exempt category:

"EXECUTIVE" - All the following conditions must be met:

a.   The employee's primary duty consists of the management of the enterprise or a recognized department therein; and
b.   The employee customarily directs the work of two or more employees; and
c.   The employee has the authority to hire or fire other employees or the employee's suggestions and recommendations on hiring, firing, advancement and promotion or any other change of status will be given particular weight; and
d.   The employee customarily and regularly exercises discretionary powers; and
e.   The employee does not devote more than 20 percent of his or her hours of work in the workweek to activities which are not directly and closely related to the performance of the work described in paragraphs (a) through (d); and
f.   The employee's salary is not less than $155 per week, exclusive of board, lodging, or other facilities. The employee's salary must be

paid for any workweek in which the employee works, regardless of the amount of time worked during the workweek.

g.   The $250 upset test may also apply. If the employee is paid at least $250 per week; the primary duty consists of management of the enterprise, division, or department; and he or she customarily and regularly directs the work of two more employees, the requirements are met.

"ADMINISTRATIVE STAFF" - All the following conditions must be met:

a. The employee's primary duty consists of either:
   (1) The performance of office or non-manual work directly related to management policies or general business operations of his or her employer,

NOTE: Routine or repetitive work does not qualify. The employee must be making, or have direct input into making, corporate policies or,

   (2) The performance of functions in the administration of a school system, or educational establishment, or of a department or recognized subdivision; and
b.   The employee customarily and regularly exercises discretion and independent judgment; and

c.
   (1) The employee regularly and directly assists a bona fide executive, or
   (2) The employee performs under only general supervision work along specialized or technical lines requiring special training, experience, or knowledge, or
   (3) The employee executes under only general supervision special assignments and tasks; and
d.   The employee does not devote more than 20 percent of his or her hours worked in the workweek to activities which are not directly and closely related to the performance of the work described in paragraphs (a) through (c); and
e.   The employee's salary is not less than $155 per week, exclusive of

board, lodging, or other facilities. The employee's salary must be paid for any workweek in which the employee works, regardless of the amount of time worked during the workweek.

f. The $250 salary upset test may also apply. If the employee is paid at least $250 per week; the primary duty consists of the performance of work described in paragraph (a) of this section which includes work requiring the exercise of discretion and independent judgment, the requirements are met.

"PROFESSIONAL" - All of the following conditions must be met:

a. The employee's primary duty consists of the performance of:
    (1) Work requiring knowledge of an advanced type in a field of science or learning customarily acquired by a prolonged course of specialized intellectual instruction and study, as distinguished from a general academic education and from an apprenticeship, and from training in the performance of routine, mental, manual, or physical processes, or
    (2) Work that is original and creative in character in a recognized field of artistic endeavor (as opposed to work which can be produced by a person endowed with general manual or intellectual ability and training), and the result of which depends primarily on the invention, imagination, or talent of the employee, or
    (3) Teaching, tutoring, instructing, or lecturing in the activity of imparting knowledge and who is employed and engaged in this activity as a teacher in the school system or educational establishment; and

b. The employee's work requires the consistent exercise of discretion and judgment in its performance; and

c. The employee's work is predominantly intellectual and varied in character (as opposed to routine mental, manual, mechanical, or physical work) and is of such character that the output produced or the result accomplished cannot be standardized in relation to a given period of time; and

d. The employee does not devote more than 20 percent of his or her hours worked in the workweek to activities which are not an essential part of and necessarily incident to the work described in paragraphs (a) through (c); and

e. The employee's salary is not less than $170 per week exclusive of board, lodging, or other facilities. The employee's salary must be paid for any workweek in which the employee works, regardless of the amount of time worked during the workweek.

f. The $250 salary upset test may also apply. If the employee is paid a salary of at least $250 per week; his or her primary duty consists of the performance either of work described in paragraph (a), (1) or (3) of this section, which includes work requiring the consistent exercise of discretion and judgment, or of work requiring invention, imagination, or talent in a recognized field of artistic endeavor, the requirements shall be deemed to be met.

By law, all employees who do not meet the criteria for "EXEMPT" are "NONEXEMPT."

"NONEXEMPT" employees include such persons as clerical, secretarial, bookkeeping, data processing, and maintenance.

"EXEMPT" employees include such persons as Administrator, Supervisor, and Ministers.

EMPLOYMENT POLICIES

1. All decisions with respect to recruitment, selection, and placement of employees shall be made on the basis of the requirements of the position to be filled and the qualifications of the individual seeking employment.

2. Every effort shall be made to bring together, in the most compatible manner, the requirements of the positions to be filled and the talents, abilities, and experience of the candidates for employment, and to afford the individual an opportunity for advancement.

3. Unless a written agreement is signed by the hiring officials of the ministry and the employee, a contractual relationship shall apply for employment with this organization.

4. Insofar as possible, vacancies shall be filled by promotion from within our organization. Notice of such vacancies shall be posted

on the bulletin board in the Administration Office. Any employee who wishes to be considered for the position may submit an application through the Human Resource Director. All applications shall be reviewed and interviews conducted by the President and the Human Resource Director, and the head of the Office or Department in which the vacancy exists.

5. When additional employees are needed in any Office or Department, the supervisor or head of the Office or Department shall submit to the Human Resource Director a written request, explaining fully the need and urgency, if any, for the additional employees.

6. Where a vacancy arises as the result of a resignation or removal of an employee, the request to fill such vacancy shall be processed promptly and without any undue delay.

7. All other requests for additional staff shall be reviewed by the President and the Human Resource Director.

8. Relatives of an employee of the ministry and members of the relative's household may be employed by Vision, provided those individuals are qualified by education and/or experience for the employment they seek.

9. Employees in this category shall be assigned to work which will not afford an opportunity for them to supervise each other, nor see each other's personnel records.

10. Former employees who left Vision in good standing may be re-employed.

11. Individuals who resigned their positions, without adequate notice, or who were dismissed for good cause, shall not be considered for re-employment.

CLASSIFICATION OF EMPLOYEES

Employees of the ministry shall be grouped into four basic classifications as follows: Full-time employees; salaried employees; part-time employees; and volunteers.

1. <u>Full-time employees:</u>

Those employees who are required to be at their jobs for a minimum of thirty-five (35) hours, and a maximum of forty (40) hours, each workweek shall be Classified as full-time employees. These employees shall be assigned to a permanent supervisor and work group.

2. <u>Salaried employees:</u>

Salaried employees are exempt from minimum wage and hour requirements. They shall be classified as Executive, Administrative, or Professional employees and shall work not less than thirty-five (35) hours each workweek.

3. <u>Part-time employees:</u>

Those employees who work on an "as needed" basis shall be classified as part-time employees. The time worked by part-time employees shall not exceed (30) hours per workweek, except in cases of emergency. When an emergency arises, the head of the Office or Department involved may authorize part-time employees to work in excess of thirty (30) hours per workweek to meet the needs of such emergencies.

4. <u>Volunteers:</u>

Those employees whose time and talents are given to the ministry without compensation shall be classified as volunteers.

PROBATIONARY APPOINTMENT

1. Each new employee shall serve a three-month probationary period. The ministry reserves the right to extend the probationary period for an additional three months, if it is deemed necessary.

2. Upon satisfactory completion of the period, the new employee shall become a full-time member of the staff of Vision unless the individual was employed specifically for a part-time or temporary position.

3. During the three-month probationary period, new employees shall not be entitled to sick leave, vacation, or holidays with pay.

4. At the completion of the probationary period, the new employee shall receive credit toward sick leave, vacation, and holidays with pay, provided the individual continues to be employed by Vision.

5. If a satisfactory position has not been found for the new employee by the end of the probationary period, employment of that individual shall be terminated.

6. Any individual whose employment is terminated during, or at the end of, the probationary period shall not be entitled to severance pay.

7. Any employee who receives an unsatisfactory efficiency rating shall be placed on probation for a period of one month, pending improvement in the performance of their assignment. Failure to receive a rating of satisfactory or better during a probationary period shall result in the dismissal of the individual.

8. Any employee who has been placed on probation shall be eligible for paid holidays, but shall not be permitted to use any vacation days during that period.

9. If an employee is absent from scheduled work while in a probationary status, that employee shall continue to serve on probation for the equivalent number of days she or he was absent from work.

10. Any individual whose employment is terminated for any reason other than "lack of work" shall not be entitled to receive accrued vacation pay.

WORKWEEK

1. Work schedules shall be established according to the needs of the ministry, the workload, and efficient personnel management.

2. The normal workweek at Vision shall begin at midnight on Sunday and end at midnight the following Sunday.

3. The normal workweek for salaried or exempt employees shall be a

234

minimum of thirty- five (35) hours or more.

4. The normal workweek for employees who work by the hour shall be thirty-five (35) hours or less.

5. All employees shall be required to work eight hours each day, with paid time off for lunch and a fifteen minute rest break.

6. The head of each Office or Department shall notify the employees assigned to that Office or Department of their daily work schedule, including lunch time, rest breaks, and changes necessitated by Vision activities.

7. When the workload of an Office or Department requires more than one 8-hour shift in one day, the head of that Office or Department shall determine the hours of work for each shift. At the earliest possible time, the head of that Office or Department shall notify the employees involved of any changes in their work schedules.

8. All employees subject to the minimum wage and hour provisions of the Fair Labor Standards Act - otherwise referred to as nonexempt employees - shall keep an individual time record, which shows the hours worked each day.

9. The following information shall be recorded on each employee's time card:

    *   Starting and quitting time for each day worked;
    *   Approval of the head of the Office or Department for work started more than fifteen (15) minutes before normal starting time and more that fifteen (15) minutes after normal quitting time;
    *   Check-out and check-in time for lunch break for each 8 hour shift;
    *   Approval of the head of each Office and Department for overtime worked by each employee is recorded on the time card and authorization by the head of the Office or Department for payment for time worked as shown on the time card.

- The head of the Office or Department shall note on the time card all paid absences, paid vacations, and paid holidays.

10. Unapproved absences shall not be considered as hours worked for pay purposes. Office and Department heads shall notify their employees whether they will receive pay for certain hours of absence.

11. Filling out the time card for another employee, or falsifying one's own time card is prohibited. Disciplinary action shall be taken and may result in termination of the employment of the individual(s) involved.

12. Executive, administrative, and professional personnel are exempt from filling out time cards and shall not receive compensation for overtime work.

COMPENSATION

1. Wages and Salaries:

Wages and salaries paid by the ministry shall be comparable to those paid by other ministries for similar work. Salary increases shall be given in recognition and appreciation of exceptional performance, and not on length of service.

2. Wage Rates:

Generally, new employees shall be paid the wage rate established for their specific work assignment and responsibilities.

3. Cost-of-living Adjustments:

During the month of December each year, wages and salaries shall be reviewed. Cost-of-living adjustments shall be considered, but shall not be made automatically.

4. Pay Day:

a. All employees of the ministry shall be paid weekly unless otherwise contracted.

5. Automatic Deductions:

On each pay day each employee shall be provided with the following information concerning automatic deductions from their pay checks:

    a. Gross amount of salary;

    b. Amount of automatic deductions for the following:

        (1) Income taxes: Federal & State.

        (2) Social Security taxes;

        (3) Insurance premiums as appropriate.

6. Overtime Compensation:

Nonexempt employees shall be paid overtime compensation for work in excess of the regular forty (40) hour workweek. Such overtime compensation shall be at the rate of one and one-half times the wage rate established for the specific work performed.

7. Vacation Pay:

All full-time and salaried employees shall be entitled to a vacation with pay. For purposes of vacations, an employee shall be considered "full-time" only if the employee is scheduled to work regularly thirty-five (35) hours or more per week.

Vacation pay shall be based on the compensation each employee receives for a regular workweek.

EMPLOYEE BENEFITS

Eligible employees at Vision are provided a wide range of benefits programs (such as workers' compensation) covering all employees by law. Since churches are exempt from most unemployment laws, their employees are normally ineligible for unemployment benefits.

Benefits eligibility is dependent upon a variety of factors, including employee classification. The Administrator can identify the programs for which each employee is eligible. Details of many of these programs can be found elsewhere in the employee handbook.

Some benefit programs require contributions from the employee, but most are fully paid by the Church.

The following benefit programs are available to eligible employees:

Auto Mileage - Mileage will be paid to personnel required to use their personal vehicles for Church errands. An expense report is required to receive the expense reimbursement. The report must include the date of business use, the destination and number of miles, and the business purpose of the trip. The rate per mile is determined by the Internal Revenue Service each year. See Section 1450 and Form F1460.

Benefit Conversion at Termination - Each employee has the right to convert his or her health insurance and disability insurance policies to private plans within 30 days of termination. Upon request, the Administrator will provide the necessary forms for the conversion. Premium payments automatically become the responsibility of the former employee.

Credit Cards - Church (company) credit cards will be issued to selected members of the staff. The use of these cards is restricted to business. Personal charges are prohibited. The cards are the responsibility of the employees to whom they are issued. These employees are responsible for providing the necessary documents and receipts to the Accounts Payable Clerk. The receipts will be matched to the monthly credit card statement, and any unsupported charges will be questioned. Each employee who accepts a card will also accept the responsibility for charges to his or her card. Any charges that cannot be supported as Church expenses must be paid to the Church or they will be deducted from the employee's pay.

Meal Allowances - The Internal Revenue Service approved rate of $26 per day for meals will be allowed while traveling on Church business. The allowance applies only when traveling on approved overnight trips. The breakdown for meals is $6 for breakfast, $8 for lunch, and $12 for dinner. Expense reports must be submitted to receive the allowance.

Medical Insurance - Group medical insurance is paid by the Church for all regular full-time employees and their families. For the regular full-time employees and/or their families who are covered by private plans, the Church pays the premium or reimburses the employee. The Church will not pay premiums on a private policy in excess of the amount that would be due for the same individual and/or his or her family in the group program.

Personal Leave - Whenever possible, requests for personal leave will be honored. The request for leave must be submitted to the Administrator. The Administrator will check the schedule and if staff scheduling will permit, the request will be put to the Board. If personal leave is granted, the employee may take any accrued sick time and vacation time he or she has available before going on unpaid leave. Vacation and Sick Leave Benefits will not continue to accrue during unpaid leave.

Tax-Sheltered Annuities - Church employees may individually purchase tax-sheltered annuities. Any employees who set up a retirement program of this type, and who desire deductions be made from their pay, must furnish their completed forms to the Payroll Clerk. The forms are provided by the agency handling the TSA. No deductions will be made for TSAs, or paid to an agency unless the completed forms are on file.

ABSENCE FROM WORK

In order to give the best possible service to our community, it is necessary for all employees of Vision to report for work regularly and to be punctual.

The ministry recognizes that circumstances beyond an employee's control may cause him or her to be late, or to be absent from work for all or part of a day. However, unauthorized absence, or tardiness, shall not be tolerated and shall be grounds for disciplinary action.

1. Paid Absences:

There are three categories of absences from work for which an employee shall be paid: a. Vacation time, b. legal holidays, and c. sick leave.

a. <u>Vacations:</u>

Upon completion of six months of continuous employment with the ministry each full-time and salaried employee shall be entitled to one calendar week's vacation with pay.

At the end of twelve consecutive months of employment, each employee shall be entitled to two calendar week's vacation with pay; and, thereafter, shall be entitled to two calendar week's vacation with pay for each succeeding year through the fourth consecutive year of employment with Vision.

Upon completion of five calendar years of continuous service with Vision, each employee shall be entitled to three calendar weeks vacation with pay each year for as long as they are employed by the ministry.

Vacations shall not be limited to the months of June, July and August. Vacations may be taken at any time during the calendar year. Vacations may not be taken until the completion of six consecutive months of employment with Vision.

Vacation time may not be carried forward into the next year of employment.

In no event shall the vacation of any employee be permitted to interrupt the responsibilities of the ministry of Vision.

Final approval of vacations shall be made by the President.

If an employee resigns or is dismissed prior to the completion of one year of service, payment for any earned, unused vacation time shall be prorated, based upon the employee's salary and length of service.

b. <u>Legal Holidays:</u>

Full-time and salaried employees of Vision shall have paid, legal holidays each year.

An official holiday which falls on Saturday shall be observed on the preceding Friday.

If the holiday falls on Sunday, it shall be observed on the following Monday.

Insofar as possible, employees of Vision shall be excused from their regular work responsibilities on these legal holidays. However, when church services of any kind are scheduled in conjunction with a legal holiday, all employees of the ministry, shall be expected to be available to render any service or minister in any way which may become necessary.

Full-time and salaried employees who have completed their probationary period shall be entitled to holiday time with pay. Part-time or temporary employees shall not be compensated for these holidays.

When a full-time or salaried employee is required, by the head of the Office or Department to which that employee is assigned, to work on an official holiday, such employee shall be granted an alternate day off with pay. The employee must take the day off or lose the privilege.

When a legal holiday falls within an employee's vacation period, an additional day of vacation shall be granted. This additional day may be taken at the beginning or at the end of the employee's vacation period; or the employee may take the time later during the year, subject to the approval of the head of the Office or Department to which the employee is assigned.

c. Sick Leave:

Employees of the ministry who have completed at least one year of service shall be eligible for sick leave with pay, based on the following conditions and limitations:

(1)The approved length of each absence because of illness shall be at the discretion of the Human Resource Director, unless otherwise provided.

(2)Paid Sick Leave.

Each employee of Vision shall be entitled to receive not more than two weeks Paid sick leave during each calendar year.

If the employee's illness continues for more than six consecutive days, the employee shall submit to the Human Resource Director a statement from the attending physician confirming the illness. The physician's statement shall be placed in the personnel file of the employee.

In the event an employee's illness extends beyond the initial two-week period, an extension of not to exceed thirty (30) days may be granted.

If an employee is unable to return to work at the expiration of the 30 day extension, the employee may return to work as soon as she or he is physically able to work, provided a vacancy exists, which the employee is qualified to fill, and the employee shall be paid the compensation authorized for that particular position.

A leave of absence may be granted to any employee whose illness or disability extends beyond the coverage provided by the Sickness Plan of the ministry, or appropriate.

(3)Maternity Leave.

The ministry shall abide by all federal and state law relating to pregnancy discrimination.

Employees on maternity leave shall be treated the same as employees on medical leave.

Additional time off may be required in maternity cases because of extenuating medical circumstances. In such cases, the Human Resource Director may grant not to exceed an additional ninety (90) days sick leave without pay. In each case, confirmation from the attending physician concerning the medical circumstances shall be taken into consideration.

(4)Sick Leave Compensation.

During any period of illness, each employee of the ministry shalt be paid the base rate of pay for eight hours per day, up to thirty-five (35) hours per week, not to exceed two weeks per calendar year.

(5)<u>Notice of Intention to Return to Work.</u>

Any employee who has been absent from work because of illness shall notify the head of his Office or Department as soon as possible the date she or he expects to return to work.

Failure to return to work on the specified date, when a suitable position is available, shall be regarded as a resignation.

2. <u>Unpaid Absences</u>

Employees are not paid for any absences which fall outside of the policies listed above. Employees may request time off work without pay. These requests must be submitted to the President and are granted or denied at his sole discretion.

PAY DEDUCTIONS AND SETOFFS

With the exception of ministers, the law requires that Vision make certain deductions from every employee's compensation, such as applicable federal income tax.

Ministers are allowed by law to choose whether they desire to have federal income tax deducted from their checks or not. If they choose to pay their own taxes quarterly, that is their right. This method also puts the full liability for failure to pay the taxes on the minister.

Since the Church has filed a Form 8274, all employees are under the Self-Employment Compensation Act. If an employee desires to have tax deducted from his or her paycheck for self-employment tax, the employee must include the extra tax on his or her completed Form W-4. The tax will be deducted and reported as federal income tax withheld.

Vision offers programs and benefits beyond those required by law. Eligible employees may voluntarily authorize deductions from their paychecks to cover the costs of participation in these programs.

Pay setoffs are pay deductions taken by Vision usually to help pay off a debt or obligation to the Church or others. The Church will not make deductions from an employee's pay, other than those required by law, unless the employee has signed an authorization form for the deduction.

Questions concerning deductions made from a paycheck, or the method used to calculate them, should be addressed to the Administrator.

ATTENDANCE AND PUNCTUALITY

1. Authorized Absence From Work.

Full-time and salaried employees shall be compensated during an authorized absence from work.

Authorized absences which exceed the number of bonus days accumulated by an employee shall be without pay, but shall not jeopardize the employment status of the employee.

Employees shall not be paid for periods of unauthorized absences. A statement from a physician may be required and shall be placed in the personnel file of the employee.

2. Notification of Anticipated Tardiness or Absence

An employee must notify the head of his Office or Department of any anticipated absence or delay in reporting for work not later than regular starting time.

If the head of that Office or Department is not available, the employee is instructed to notify the Human Resource Director, who, in turn, shall pass the information on to the appropriate Office or Department.

3. Disciplinary Action for Noncompliance.

Failure on the part of any employee to notify the ministry in accordance with this policy may result in loss of compensation for the absence and may be grounds for disciplinary action.

4. <u>Attendance Record.</u>

An employee's attendance record shall be considered in determining whether to recommend a salary increase or promotion for that employee.

5. <u>Death in the Family</u>

In the event of a death in the immediate family of an employee, a leave of absence for not to exceed three (3) days shall be granted to such employee as "Bonus Days."

6. <u>Weather Conditions.</u>

If the ministry is open and does not declare an emergency closing because of inclement weather conditions, all employees shall be expected to make a good-faith effort to report to work. Those employees who are unable to report for work during inclement weather conditions shall be granted an authorized, but unpaid, absence.

<u>BONUS DAYS</u>

1. All full-time and salaried employees of Vision shall be eligible to earn, with pay, one bonus day per calendar quarter.

2. These bonus days may be used for any purpose, at any time, with the approval of the head of the Office or Department to which the employee is assigned.

3. Bonus days may be accumulated up to a total of not more than seven (7) days and may be carried over from year to year.

MILITARY LEAVE OF ABSENCE

1. <u>Requirements for Military Leave of Absence.</u>

A military leave of absence shall be granted to any following criteria:

a. Enlists in the Armed Forces of the United States.

b. Is inducted into any branch of the Armed Forces through the

Selective Service System.

c. Serves on either active or inactive duty with the Armed Forces while she or he is a member of a Reserve Unit.

2. Active Military Duty Without Pay.

An employee of Vision who serves on active military duty for more than two weeks shall not be paid by the ministry while on a military leave of absence.

3. Active Military Duty With Pay.

An employee of the ministry who has completed one year of service with Vision shall be paid her or his regular salary, less military pay, during the period of active military service, provided the employee is a member of the Armed Forces Reserves and has been granted a military leave of absence by the ministry to serve on active duty for not more than two weeks.

CONFIDENTIALITY

Employees of Vision are required to keep in strict confidence all information concerning the personal lives of people in the community.

Information concerning charitable contributions and confidences, which are shared during spiritual counseling, are privileged information, and employees are required to hold such knowledge in strictest confidence.

It is the nature of Christian service that employees gain intimate knowledge of the lives of people in the community. These people depend on the employees to respect and protect their privacy.

Only with the express, written authorization of the President may information be released through the media and thus become public knowledge.

A signed release is required for all endorsements.

Information about the ministries' internal activities should also be treated carefully. Although many of the activities are not confidential, others are and they should not be made public except when the President and/or Board of Directors/Regents officially decide to release such information. A staff member should never speak directly to a government official or municipal representative or to the media about affairs at the ministry. Any such inquiry should receive a very polite: "I'm sorry, I'm not qualified to answer that question. I will refer you to my supervisor."

Each member of the staff is obligated to personally uphold the following promise:

"As a member of the Vision staff, I pledge that I shall respect and maintain the confidential relationships that exist among the Ministry, Board of Directors, Ministers, and each of its members or friends. I shall not discuss nor reveal counseling conversations, personal information, transactions or negotiations involving our members or friends with others persona. I will not reveal information disclosing the Ministries' internal activities. Only when authorized by the President of the Board of Directors/Regents shall I disclose any of the above information." Any breach of this confidentially shall be cause for dismissal.

OUTSIDE EMPLOYMENT

Full-time employees of Vision may not accept outside employment without the consent of the Human Resource Director.

Vision recognizes that circumstances may make it necessary for an employee to consider outside employment. However, the employee's right to do as she or he wishes during off-hours must be balanced against the need of the Ministry for a productive, alert employee at all times.

No employee shall accept outside employment with any business which, by its nature, may be harmful to the image of Vision in the community or may be in conflict with the interests of Vision.

Outside employment shall not be accepted by the Ministry as an excuse for:

1. Poor performance;

2. Tardiness;

3. Absenteeism;

4. Refusal to work overtime.

Should any of these situations occur, permission to accept outside employment shall be withdrawn.

CODE OF ETHICS AND PERSONAL CONDUCT

In 1 Thessalonians Chapter 3:21-22, the Apostle Paul admonishes the people to "Prove all things; hold fast to that which is good. Abstain from all appearance of evil."

In Colossians1:10-12, the Apostle Paul urges the people to,

"walk worthy of the Lord unto all pleasing, being fruitful in every good work, and increasing in the knowledge of God; Strengthened with all might according to his glorious power, unto all patience and long-suffering with joyfulness; Giving thanks unto the Father, which hath made us meet to be partakers of the inheritance of the saints in light."

Using these scriptures as guidelines for our personal conduct, the staff of Vision is expected to maintain its personal affairs in a sound, moral, and ethical manner, and to live a Christian life which will reflect with honor on the reputation of the Ministry.

The staff of Vision shall conduct their personal lives in a manner which:

1. Is consistent with their obligations to family and relatives.

2. Does not violate moral, ethical, and Christian standards within the community.

3. Recognizes and respects the personal and property rights of others.

Vision encourages its employees to participate in community and political activities which do not interfere with the responsibilities and obligations of their employment with the Ministry and to make it clear that they do not speak on behalf of Vision.

DRESS CODE

All employees of the Ministry shall maintain the highest standard of personal cleanliness and grooming during working hours, and shall present a neat, business-like appearance at all times. Every employee will have some contact with the public, and in her or his appearance and actions will represent the Ministry.

Conduct and dress in the ministry are also a part of the courtesy we owe to those who work with us.

Employees are expected to dress in a manner that is normally accepted in professional business establishments which provide service to the public.

Examples of dress and grooming which are not acceptable are as follows:

Extremes of any style

See-through or transparent clothing

Torn or frayed clothing

Soiled clothing

Dresses or blouses with bare midriffs or backless tops

Hair, mustaches, and sideburns which are not neatly trimmed

If any employee reports for work improperly dressed or groomed, the head of the Office or Department to which the employee is assigned shall instruct the employee to return home, change clothes, and take any other appropriate action which may be needed. The employee shall not be compensated during such time away from work.

Repeated violations of this dress code shall be cause for termination of employment.

CONDUCT

Moral/Spiritual/Professional

All staff members are expected to conduct themselves in the highest order of moral, spiritual and professional conduct. We are to individually endeavor to be as Jesus Christ would want us to be. Each staff member should seek to become acquainted with all areas of ministry and service within the ministry. Staff members must meet all membership requirements and be members of a church. Also, it is paramount that each staff member treat one another with courtesy and understanding, being in submission to one another, just as Christ would. A friendly greeting, a smile, a willing and tender spirit, and a positive attitude is essential. Let Jesus Christ shine through you!

All staff members are expected to conduct themselves in the highest professional standards and manner. All staff members are expected to engage in mutual and cooperative actions in relationships, not only with other staff members, but also with leaders.

Murmuring, gossiping, poor communication, profanity, and lack of submission to authority will not be allowed. When a misunderstanding arises among staff members, do not relate this misunderstanding to another staff member. Rather follow the procedure outlined in Matthew 18: 15-17. If, after going to the "offending" staff member personally, you cannot resolve the misunderstanding, go to your supervisor immediately so that the problem may be resolved. Do not allow misunderstandings or inter-office conflicts to remain in your heart but resolve them prayerfully and scripturally so that unity and love can permeate our relationships together. The use of tobacco or any chemical substance will be cause for immediate dismissal from the staff.

BUSINESS TRAVEL EXPENSES

Vision will reimburse employees for reasonable business travel expenses incurred while on assignments away from the Church. All business travel must be approved in advance by the Administrator or Board.

Employees whose travel plans have been approved should make all travel arrangements through the Church's designated travel agency.

When approved, the actual costs of travel, meals, lodging, and other expenses directly related to accomplishing business travel objectives will be reimbursed by Vision. Employees are expected to limit expenses to reasonable amounts.

Employees who are involved in an accident while traveling on business must promptly report the incident to their immediate supervisor.

Vehicles owned, leased, or rented by Vision may not be used for personal use.

Cash advances to cover reasonable anticipated expenses may be made to employees, after travel has been approved. Employees should submit a written request to their supervisor when travel advances are needed. Anyone receiving a travel advance will also be required to sign an authorization that all or part of the advance may be deducted from the employee's pay if the employee fails to provide the necessary documentation to prove business use of the advance within 30 days.

When travel is completed, employees must submit completed travel expense reports within 30 days. Reports should be accompanied by receipts for all individual expenses whenever possible. Some expenses of $25 or less will be allowed even if no receipt is available. However, these expenses must be fully explained and there must be a valid reason for the lack of a receipt.

Employees should contact the Administrator for guidance and assistance on procedures related to travel arrangements, travel advances, expense reports, reimbursement for specific expenses, or any other business travel issues.

Abuse of this business travel expense policy, including falsifying expense reports to reflect costs not incurred by the employee, can be grounds for disciplinary action, up to and including termination of employment.

BUSINESS GIFTS AND ENTERTAINMENT

Gifts - The Internal Revenue Service limits business gifts to any business associate to $25 per year.

Vision must use caution in the purchase of such gifts. Since the Church is a nonprofit organization, the excess spent above $25 for a gift could be classified by the Internal Revenue Service as an expenditure not for an exempt purpose. This could jeopardize the Church's exempt status.

Business gifts must be substantiated. A receipt is required stating the cost of the gift and the date purchased. Also, the name of the person receiving the gift, the business reason for the gift, and the business relationship of the recipient must be noted.

Gifts to employees of more than a minimum amount are taxable compensation to the employee and must be added to the employee's wages.

Entertainment - The cost of meals or entertainment must be directly related to, or associated with, the active conduct of business. These expenses must be fully documented. They must be supported by receipts. Also, a written explanation of each of the following is required:

(1) The name(s) of the person(s) involved.
(2) The type of activity must be stated.
(3) The reason for the meal or entertainment.
(4) The location of the meal or entertainment, including the place of the business discussion if the expense is associated with, instead of directly related to, the Church's business or exempt purpose.
(5) The date and time of the meal or entertainment, as well as the duration of the business discussion if the expense is associated with, instead of directly related to the Church's business or exempt purpose.

Meals or entertainment may be provided to employees, or employees and their families occasionally without being considered as taxable compensation. The same types of documentation are required.

LUNCH AND REST BREAKS

Each full-time and salaried employee of the ministry shall be permitted to take not to exceed thirty (30) minutes for lunch near the middle of the work-day. From time to time it may be necessary to adjust the lunch period, depending on the workload and needs of the Office or Department to which the employee is assigned.

The head of the Office or Department shall schedule the lunch period for the employees under her or his supervision.

No employee shall work more than five (5) consecutive hours without taking time away from work to have a meal.

A kitchen is provided for the use of the employees. It is equipped with a refrigerator, microwave oven, double sink, limited cabinet space, and a trash can. Each employee who uses the kitchen shall be held responsible for leaving the facilities neat and clean after each use.

Employees shall not prolong their lunch period beyond the authorized maximum of thirty (30) minutes and their rest period beyond the permitted fifteen (15) minutes without the approval of the head of their Office or Department.

PERSONAL TELEPHONE CALLS AND PERSONAL MAIL

1. Personal Telephone Calls
The telephone lines of Vision shall be used for official business. Employees may make minimal personal phone calls as necessary.

2. Personal Mail

Vision employees shall be permitted to use the address of the ministry to receive their personal mail.

DRUGS, NARCOTICS, ALCOHOL AND TOBACCO

Vision prohibits the use, sale, dispensing, or possession of illegal drugs, narcotics, alcoholic beverages, and tobacco on its premises. This prohibition covers all legal or prescription drugs which may impair the ability of an employee to carry out his or her work assignment.

1. Disciplinary action.

Vision shall take appropriate action against employees who have in their possession or are under the influence of alcohol or illegal drugs while on the premises of the ministry.

2. Employees Who Report to Work Under the Influence.

An employee who reports to work under the influence of drugs, narcotics, or alcohol shall not be permitted to remain on the premises of the ministry. Any employee found to be under the influence of drugs, narcotics, or alcohol during working hours shall be required to leave the premises and shall be escorted home.

3. Employees Who Bring Un-prescribed Drugs, Narcotics, or Alcohol to Work.

Any employee who brings un-prescribed drugs, narcotics, or alcoholic beverages to work and uses them on the Vision premises or dispenses or sells them on the Vision premises shall be subject to disciplinary action up to and including termination of their employment.

4. Use of Prescribed Drugs or Narcotics During Working Hours.

Any employee who must use prescribed drugs or narcotics during working hours shall be required to determine that the effects of the drug or narcotic will not create a potential safety risk while performing her or his work assignment.

5. Counseling for Employees With Drug-Related Problems.

Any employee who experiences problems resulting from drug, narcotic, or alcohol abuse or dependency shall be instructed to seek counseling. Such counseling shall be kept confidential and shall not influence the employee's efficiency rating. Job performance alone shall be the basis of all efficiency ratings and not the fact that an employee has sought counseling.

6. Medical Examination

The head of any Office or Department who notices an employee demonstrating unusual behavior patterns, which appear to be drug, narcotic, or alcohol related, shall, in consultation with the Human

Resource Director, arrange to have that individual examined by a physician or at a clinic to determine whether she or he has become addicted.

7. <u>Rehabilitation.</u>

Any employee who has been diagnosed by a qualified physician as being addicted to drugs or alcohol may be granted a leave of absence to undertake rehabilitation treatment. Such employee shall not be permitted to return to work until such employee presents to the Human Resource Director a statement, certifying that the employee has been rehabilitated and is capable of performing the work normally assigned to him.

GRIEVANCES

The procedure for handling matters involving Employee-Employer Relations shall be as follows:

Employees are invited to discuss suggestions, questions, complaints, or problems with the Human Resource Director.

However, there may be times when an employee prefers not to discuss a problem with the Human Resource Director. If the matter is of such a personal or confidential nature that the employee can discuss it with the Human Resource Director, or she or he may go directly to the President.

A complete written record of the problem and its resolution shall be maintained by the Human Resource Director.

Recourse or retaliation against an employee who has brought a problem or complaint to the attention of the President shall be prohibited.

DISCIPLINARY ACTION

It is the policy of Vision to provide a procedure for fair and equitable discipline for all employees and, where appropriate, to allow for corrective guidance in order to achieve a satisfactory level of performance and/or conduct.

The Human Resource Director shall have the responsibility for determining the type of disciplinary action to be taken.

Disciplinary action for all employees may consist of any one or all of the following:

1. Warnings - oral or written
2. Counseling
3. Reprimands
4. Suspensions
5. Probation
6. Termination of employment

SUMMARY OF EMPLOYEE BENEFITS

1. Hospitalization

After an individual has been employed by the Ministry for sixty (60) days, the Ministry provides, at its expense, hospitalization insurance for all full-time employees who work thirty-five (35) hours or more per workweek.

2. Dental Insurance

After an individual has been employed by the Ministry for sixty (60) days, the Ministry also provides at its expense Dental insurance for all full-time and salaried employees who work thirty-five (35) hours or more per workweek.

3. Bonus Days

For every calendar quarter in which an employee has a perfect attendance record, she or he shall receive one (1) bonus day. See the section on "Bonus Days" for further details.

4. Vacations

All full-time and salaried employees who work thirty-five (35) hours or more, per workweek, shall be entitled to a paid vacation as set forth in the section on "Vacations."

To assure accurate records for payroll and benefit purposes, each employee shall furnish to the Human Resource Director in writing the following information and shall keep the information current:

EMPLOYEE'S PERSONNEL FILE

1. Address and telephone number

2. Name, address and telephone number of nearest relative or person to notify in case of emergency

3. Legal change of name

4. Change of marital status for insurance purposes

5. Birth or adoption of a child

6. Change of beneficiary for insurance purposes

7. Change in number of dependents

8. Death of a member of the family

JOB

Your job is an important ministry, not only to you, but to those responsible for overseeing the activities of the Ministry. This Ministry has a responsibility to its employees in establishing personnel policies and practices that will enlist the loyalty and support of every employee.

As an employee, you too have a responsibility to your work, that of performing your job in the best and most efficient manner of which you are capable. The success of the Ministry staff is not the result of the efforts of a few, but of the combined teamwork of every person from the eldest to the newest employee dedicated to this Ministry.

REQUIRED MEETINGS

They are required of all the ministry team of Vision. They are:

Staff meetings - As required.

Annual Ministry Team Advance - Annual as required.

DISABILITY ACCOMMODATION

Vision is committed to complying fully with the Americans with Disabilities Act (ADA) and ensuring equal opportunity in employment for qualified persons with disabilities. All employment practices and activities are conducted on a nondiscriminatory basis.

Hiring procedures have been reviewed and provide persons with disabilities meaningful employment opportunities. Assistance in completing job applications is available upon request. Pre-employment inquiries are made only regarding an applicant's ability to perform the duties of the position.

Reasonable accommodation is available to all disabled employees, where their disability affects the performance of job functions. All employment decisions are based on the merits of the situation in accordance with defined criteria, not the disability of the individual.

Qualified individuals with disabilities are entitled to equal pay and other forms of compensation (or changes in compensation) as well as in job assignments, classifications, organizational structures, position descriptions, lines of progression, and seniority lists. Leave of all types will be available to all employees on an equal basis.

The Organization is also committed to not discriminating against any qualified employees or applicants because they are related to or associated with a person with a disability. The Organization will follow any state or local law that provides individuals with disabilities greater protection than the ADA.

This policy is neither exhaustive nor exclusive. Vision is committed to taking all other actions necessary to ensure equal employment opportunity for persons with disabilities in accordance with the ADA and all other applicable federal, state, and local laws.

IMMIGRATION LAW COMPLIANCE

Vision is committed to employing only United States citizens and aliens who are authorized to work in the United States and does not unlawfully discriminate on the basis of citizenship or national origin.

In compliance with the Immigration Reform and Control Act of 1986, each new employee, as a condition of employment, must complete the Employment Eligibility Verification Form 1-9 and present documentation establishing identity and employment eligibility. Former employees who are rehired must also complete the form if they have not completed an I-9 with the Organization within the past three years, or if their previous I-9 is no longer retained or valid.

Employees with questions or seeking more information on immigration law issues are encouraged to contact the Administrator. Employees may raise questions or complaints about immigration law compliance without fear of reprisal.

CONFLICTS OF INTEREST

Employees have an obligation to conduct business within guidelines that prohibit actual or potential conflicts of interest. This policy establishes only the framework within which Vision wishes the Organization to operate. The purpose of these guidelines is to provide general direction so that employees can seek further clarification on issues related to the subject of acceptable standards of operation. Contact the Administrator for more information or questions about conflicts of interest.

An actual or potential conflict of interest occurs when an employee is in a position to influence a decision that may result in a personal gain for that employee or for a relative as a result of Vision's business dealings. For the purposes of this policy, a relative is any person who is related by blood or marriage, or whose relationship with the employee is similar to that of persons who are related by blood or marriage.

No "presumption of guilt" is created by the mere existence of a relationship with outside firms. However, if employees have any influence on transactions involving purchases, contracts, or leases, it is imperative that they disclose to the Administrator of the Organization as soon as possible the existence of any actual or potential conflict of interest so that safeguards can be established to protect all parties.

Personal gain may result not only in cases where an employee or relative has a significant ownership in a firm with which Vision does business, but also when an employee or relative receives any kickback, bribe, substantial gift, or special consideration as a result of any transaction or business dealings involving the Organization.

EMPLOYMENT OF MINORS

Vision recognizes that special federal employment regulations apply to children under the age of 18.

Age 18 is the minimum age for jobs declared to be particularly hazardous. These jobs include such things as driving a motor vehicle, using power tools, operating lawn mowers, saws, knives, etc.

Age 16 is the minimum age for most jobs. Jobs involving any of the items listed in the preceding paragraph are not permitted.

Age 14 is the minimum age in a limited number of jobs. An individual aged 14 or 15 may work in an office performing clerical work or work in the nursery. Individuals in this age group may also do work such as dusting and cleaning and some work on the grounds. They may not use any equipment that could cause injury, nor may they climb, or be exposed to chemicals that may be hazardous to their health.

Minors 14 or 15 are also limited in the hours they may work. The following conditions must be met:

a) All work must be performed outside school hours.
b) When school is in session, they may work a maximum of 3 hours per day and 18 hours per week.
c) When school is not in session, they may work a maximum of 8 hours per day and 40 hours per week.
d) All work must be performed between 7 a.m. and 7 p.m. from the day after Labor Day through May 31.
e) All work must be performed between 7 a.m. and 9 p.m. from June 1 through Labor Day.

Children under the age of 14 may not be employed.

Federal regulations for the employment of minors are overridden by state regulations when the state regulations are more stringent than federal.

EMPLOYMENT APPLICATIONS

Vision International relies upon the accuracy of information contained in the employment application, as well as the accuracy of other data presented throughout the hiring process and employment. Any misrepresentations, falsifications, or material omissions in any of this information or data may result in the organization's exclusion of the individual from further consideration for employment or, if the person has been hired, termination of employment.

EMPLOYMENT REFERENCE CHECKS

To ensure that individuals hired by Vision are well qualified and have a strong potential to be productive and successful, it is the policy of the organization to check the employment references of all applicants. Vision's application for employment contains the applicant's authorization for the inquiry.

REQUESTS FOR INFORMATION ON EMPLOYEES

The Administrator will respond in writing only to those reference check inquiries that are submitted in writing. Responses to such inquiries will confirm only dates of employment, wage rates, and position(s) held. No employment data will be released without a written authorization and release signed by the individual who is the subject of the inquiry.

INTRODUCTORY PERIOD

The introductory period is intended to give new employees the opportunity to demonstrate their ability to achieve a satisfactory level of performance and to determine whether the new position meets their expectations. Vision uses this period to evaluate employee capabilities, work habits, and overall performance. Either the employee or the Organization may end the employment relationship at will at any time during or after the introductory period, with or without cause or advance notice.

All new and re-hired employees work on an introductory basis for the first 90 calendar days after their date of hire. Any significant absence will automatically extend an introductory period by the length of the absence. If Vision determines that the designated introductory period does not allow sufficient time to thoroughly evaluate the employee's performance, the introductory period may be extended for a specified period.

Upon satisfactory completion of the introductory period, an employee enters the "regular" employment classification. A Payroll Change Notice will be completed by the employee's supervisor stating the change in status. After the change has been approved, the employee will receive a copy of the notice.

ACCESS TO PERSONNEL FILES

Vision maintains a personnel file on each employee. The personnel file includes such information as the employee's job application, resume, records of training, documentation of performance appraisals and salary increases, and other employment records.

Personnel files are the property of Vision and access to the information they contain is restricted. Generally, only the Administrator, Supervisors and Board-members who have a legitimate reason to review information in a file are allowed to do so.

Employees who wish to review their own files should contact the Administrator. With one week's advance notice, employees may review their own personnel files in the Organization's offices and in the presence of an individual appointed by Vision to maintain the files. Should the employee desire a copy of some of the items in the file, the request will be granted within reasonable limits. An employee may review his or her file no more than once per year.

PERSONNEL DATA CHANGES

It is the responsibility of each employee to promptly notify Vision of any changes in personnel data. Personal mailing addresses, telephone numbers, number and names of dependents, and individuals to be contacted in the event of an emergency should be accurate and current at all times. When personnel data changes, notify the Administrator.

A new Form W-4 must be completed for any changes to an employee's name, address, marital status, or number of dependents.

Each employee should complete new forms so Vision will have the information needed for federal reports and for various insurance programs. When a change of personnel data occurs, please complete the required forms so the Organization's records will be current.

All information is confidential and will be kept in the employee's personnel file.

PERFORMANCE EVALUATION

Supervisors and employees are strongly encouraged to discuss job performance and goals on an informal, day-to-day basis. A formal written performance evaluation will be conducted at the end of an employee's initial period of hire, known as the introductory period. Additional formal performance evaluations are conducted to provide both supervisors and employees the opportunity to discuss job tasks, identify and correct weaknesses, encourage and recognize strengths, and discuss positive, purposeful approaches for meeting goals.

The performance of all employees is generally evaluated according to an ongoing 12-month cycle, in time for the calendar-year-end budget estimates.

Merit-based pay adjustments are awarded by Vision in an effort to recognize truly superior employee performance. The decision to award such an adjustment is dependent upon numerous factors, including the information documented by this formal performance evaluation process.

EMPLOYEE PERFORMANCE EVALUATION

INSTRUCTIONS

WHEN IS REVIEW REQUIRED?

(a) Annual review to be conducted by December 31 each year.
(b) Introductory employee review after 90 days.
(c) Terminated employee review for personnel file.
(d) Review can be done any time, or when an employee has performed especially well, or when an employee's performance falls below standard.

WHO SHOULD PREPARE REVIEW?

(a) The employee's supervisor.
(b) If an employee works for more than one supervisor, each should complete a form (c) The Board.

RATING SYSTEM:

"E"   Excellent. Employee performs all tasks in an exceptional manner and requires little or no supervision.

"G"   Good. Employee performs many tasks well, all other tasks adequately, and requires little or no supervision.

"S"   Satisfactory. Employee performs all tasks satisfactorily and requires normal supervision.

"F"   Fair. Employee performs most tasks satisfactorily but not all and requires more than normal supervision.

"U"   Unsatisfactory. Employee fails to perform many tasks and requires close and constant supervision.

OVERALL RATING:
The reviewer's overall impression of the employee. This may or may not be an average or summation of the rated characteristics.

GENERAL COMMENTS:

In your own words, sum up the employee's strengths, weaknesses, and suggestions to employee for improvement. Also include the employee's potential for increased responsibility and job promotion. If additional space is required, use the back of the form.

REVIEW:

All forms should be reviewed by the Administrator.

The report should be discussed with the employee so the individual will know how well he or she is doing his or her job. The employee's signature on the report is only verification that the evaluation has been discussed with him or her. It does not mean the employee agrees or disagrees with anything included in the evaluation. Once the evaluation has been discussed and signed, a copy should be given to the employee. No later than three working days after the employee is given a copy of the evaluation, the employee may submit a written commentary or rebuttal. The employee's statement is to be stapled to the evaluation form and both are then filed together.

SICK LEAVE BENEFITS

Vision provides paid sick leave benefits to all eligible employees for periods of temporary absence due to illnesses or injuries. Eligible employee classifications:

Regular full-time employees.
Regular part-time employees.

Eligible employees will accrue sick leave benefits at the rate of 6 days per year (one-half of one day for every full month of service). Sick leave benefits are calculated on the basis of a "benefit year," the 12-month period that begins when the employee starts to earn sick leave benefits.

Paid sick leave can be used in minimum increments of one day. Eligible employees may use sick leave benefits for an absence due to their own illness or injury or that of a family member who resides in the employee's household.

Employees who are unable to report to work due to illness or injury must contact the office at the scheduled start of their workday if possible. The office must also be contacted on each additional day of absence.

Sick leave benefits will be calculated based on the employee's base pay rate at the time of absence and will not include any special forms of compensation, such as incentives or bonuses.

Unused sick leave benefits will not be allowed to accumulate from one year to the next. Any unused sick leave benefits will be lost at December 31 each year. On January 1 a new benefit year will begin. Employees who have worked the preceding December will receive their accrual of sick time from that month for a maximum of 4 hours.

Sick leave benefits are intended solely to provide income protection in the event of illness or injury, and may not be used for any other absence. Unused sick leave benefits will not be paid to employees while they are employed or upon termination of employment, unless required by state law.

TIME OFF TO VOTE

Vision encourages employees to fulfill their civic responsibilities by participating in elections. Generally, employees are able to find time to vote either before or after their regular work schedule. If employees are unable to vote in an election during their non-working hours, the Organization will grant up to one hour of paid time off to vote.

Employees should request time off to vote from their supervisor at least two working days prior to the election day. Advance notice is required so that the necessary time off can be scheduled at the beginning or end of the work shift, whichever provides the least disruption to the normal work schedule.

BEREAVEMENT LEAVE

Employees who wish to take time off due to the death of an immediate family member should notify their supervisor immediately.

Up to three days of paid bereavement leave will be provided to eligible employees in the following classifications:

Regular full-time employees.
Regular part-time employees.

Paid bereavement leave for a regular part-time employee will be determined by dividing the time the employee works per week by the time a regular full-time employee works per week. This ratio will be applied to the maximum of three days paid leave allowed for regular full-time employees.

Bereavement pay is calculated based on the base pay rate at the time of absence and will not include any special forms of compensation, such as incentives or bonuses.

Approval of bereavement leave may be requested by telephone, if necessary. Employees may, with their supervisor's approval, use any available paid leave for additional time off as necessary.

Vision defines "immediate family" as the employee's spouse, parents, grandparents, children, grandchildren, or siblings; the employee's spouse's parents, children, or siblings; and the employee's child's spouse.

JURY DUTY

Vision encourages employees to fulfill their civic responsibilities by serving jury duty when required. Employees in an eligible classification may request up to two weeks of paid jury duty leave over any two-year period.

Jury duty pay will be calculated on the employee's base pay rate times the number of hours the employee would otherwise have worked on the day(s) of absence. Employee classifications that qualify for paid jury duty leave are:

Regular full-time employees.
Regular part-time employees.

Jury duty pay for a regular part-time employee will be pro-rated to the maximum allowed for a regular full-time employee by dividing the time worked by a regular full-time employee into the time worked by the regular part-time employee.

If employees are required to serve jury duty beyond the period of paid jury duty leave, they may use any available paid time off (for example, vacation benefits) or may request an unpaid leave of absence.

Employees must show the jury duty summons to their supervisor as soon as possible so that the supervisor may make arrangements to accommodate their absence. Of course, employees are expected to report for work whenever the court schedule permits.

Either Vision or the employee may request an excuse from jury duty if, in the Organization's judgment, the employee's absence would create serious operational difficulties.

The Organization will continue to provide health insurance benefits for the full term of the jury duty absence.

Vacation, sick leave, and holiday benefits will continue to accrue during unpaid leave.

Since the fee paid by the county for jury duty is minimal, the employee is not required to turn it over to the Organization.

TIMEKEEPING

Accurately recording time worked is the responsibility of every nonexempt employee. Federal and state laws require Vision to keep an accurate record of time worked in order to calculate employee pay and benefits. Time worked is all the time actually spent on the job performing assigned duties.

Nonexempt employees should accurately record the time they begin and end their work, as well as the beginning and ending time of each meal period. They should also record the beginning and ending time of any split shift or departure from work for personal reasons. Overtime work must always be approved before it is performed.

Altering, falsifying, tampering with time records, or recording time on another employee's time record may result in disciplinary action, up to and including termination of employment.

Nonexempt employees should report to work no more than seven minutes prior to their scheduled starting time nor stay more than seven minutes after their scheduled stop time without prior authorization from their supervisor.

Each employee is responsible for signing his or her time record to certify the accuracy of all time recorded before submitting it for payroll processing.

SEXUAL AND OTHER UNLAWFUL HARASSMENT

Vision is committed to providing a work environment that is free of discrimination and unlawful harassment. Actions, words, jokes, or comments based on an individual's sex, race, ethnicity, age, religion, or any other legally protected characteristic will not be tolerated. As an example, sexual harassment (both overt and subtle) is a form of employee misconduct that is demeaning to another person, undermines the integrity of the employment relationship, and is strictly prohibited.

Any employee who wants to report an incident of sexual or other unlawful harassment should promptly report the matter to his or her supervisor. If the supervisor is unavailable or the employee believes it would be inappropriate to contact that person, the employee should immediately contact the Administrator or a member of the Board. Employees can raise concerns and make reports without fear of reprisal.

Any supervisor or manager who becomes aware of possible sexual or other unlawful harassment should promptly advise the Administrator or a Boardmember who will handle the matter in a timely and confidential manner.

Anyone engaging in sexual or other unlawful harassment action will be disciplined, up to and including termination of employment.

DRUG TESTING

Vision is committed to providing a safe, efficient, and productive work environment for all employees. Using or being under the influence of drugs or alcohol on the job may pose serious safety and health risks. To help ensure a safe and healthful working environment, job applicants and employees may be asked to provide body substance samples (such as urine, hair, and/or blood) to determine the illicit or illegal use of drugs and alcohol. Refusal to submit to drug testing may result in disciplinary action, up to and including termination of employment.

The ministerial staff will provide confidential counseling and referral services to employees for assistance with such problems as drug and/or alcohol abuse or addiction. It is the employee's responsibility to seek assistance prior to reaching a point where he or she will be subject to disciplinary judgment, performance, or where the behavior has led to imminent disciplinary action. Requests for assistance after the disciplinary process has begun may not preclude disciplinary action, up to and including termination of employment.

Copies of the drug testing policy will be provided to all employees. Employees will be asked to sign an acknowledgment form indicating that they have received a copy of the drug testing policy. Questions concerning this policy or its administration should be directed to the Administrator.

DRUG TESTING POLICY
EMPLOYEES' ACKNOWLEDGEMENT

Vision desires to provide a drug-free, healthful, and safe workplace. Therefore, no employee may use, possess, distribute, sell, or be under the influence of alcohol or illegal drugs while on the organization's property or while conducting business-related activities. Failure to comply with this rule may result in immediate dismissal.

Our organization reserves the right to test job applicants or current employees for drugs. Should our organization choose to exercise this right, the individual could be asked to submit to medical tests of hair, blood, or urine. Vision will pay any employee his or her normal wage while he or she is being tested. The organization will also pay the testing fees.

If a drug test produces a positive result, the applicant or employee will be asked to submit to a test by a different method. Should the second test be reported as positive, the applicant will not be hired, and if the test is on an employee, he or she may be immediately discharged.

Vision does not intend this policy as an accusation of alcohol or illegal drug use. As an employer, however, the organization has an obligation to protect the rights of the Organization and of its employees.

I have read and understand the alcohol and illegal drug policy shown above. As an employee of Vision I agree to abide by the policy as written.

I also understand the Organization will ask for my written permission for drug testing and the release of the results of such tests before a test is performed. Should a drug test ever be requested, I agree to provide the necessary permission.

Employee's Signature _____ Date _____

Signature of Witness _____Date _____

EMPLOYEE'S CONSENT FOR DRUG TESTING

EXAMPLE FORM

I agree to Vision's request for a drug test. I understand this request for a drug test is not an accusation, but desire to assure my employer that I am abiding by the Organization's policy against alcohol and illegal drug abuse as stated on Form 1540F.

I authorize the testing facility to release the test results to Vision's Administrator. If a test should prove positive, I agree to a second test by a different method.

All costs for the tests will be paid by Vision and the Organization will pay my normal wages for the time required for the testing.

Employee's Signature _____ Date _____

Signature of Witness _____Date _____

EMPLOYMENT - TERMINATION

Termination of employment is an inevitable part of personnel activity within any organization, and many of the reasons for termination are routine. Below are examples of some of the most common circumstances under which employment is terminated:

RESIGNATION - voluntary employment termination initiated by an employee.

DISCHARGE - involuntary employment termination initiated by the organization.

LAYOFF - involuntary employment termination initiated by the organization for non-disciplinary reasons.

RETIREMENT - voluntary employment termination initiated by the employee for retirement from the organization and from the work force in general.

Since employment with Vision International University is based on mutual consent, both the employee and the Organization have the right to terminate employment at will, with or without cause, at any time.

Employee benefits will be affected by employment termination in the following manner. All accrued, vested benefits that are due and payable at termination will be paid. Some benefits may be continued at the employee's expense if the employee so chooses. All sick leave and vacation leave benefits will be lost at the time of termination, unless prohibited by state law. The employee may request the necessary forms for continuing his or her various insurance programs from the Administrator.

VISITORS IN THE WORKPLACE

To provide for the safety and security of employees and the facilities at Vision, only authorized visitors are allowed in the building. Restricting unauthorized visitors helps maintain safety standards, protects against theft, ensures security of equipment, protects confidential information, safeguards employee welfare, and avoids potential distractions and disturbances.

All visitors should enter Vision at the office reception area. Authorized visitors will receive directions or be escorted to their destination. Employees are responsible for the conduct and safety of their visitors.

If an unauthorized individual is observed on premises, employees should immediately notify the Administrator or, if necessary, direct the individual to the reception area.

Any deviation from the above rules must be approved by the Administrator.

PETTY CASH

In the interest of safety, no petty cash fund will be kept by the Organization.

All transactions will be by charge or check.

The Administrator and the Controller may jointly sign checks up to a maximum of $2500.

All checks for more than $2500 must be co-signed by a Board-member.

WORKERS' COMPENSATION INSURANCE

Vision provides a comprehensive workers' compensation insurance program at no cost to employees. This program covers any injury or illness sustained in the course of employment that requires medical, surgical, or hospital treatment. Subject to applicable legal requirements, workers' compensation insurance provides benefits after a seven-day waiting period from the date of the work related injury or illness.

Employees who sustain work-related injuries or illnesses should inform their supervisor immediately. The injury or illness must also be reported immediately to the Administrator. No matter how minor an on-the-job injury may appear, it is important that it be reported immediately. This will enable an eligible employee to qualify for coverage as quickly as possible.

When an employee is absent due to a covered injury or illness, the employee's vacation and sick leave benefits will continue to accrue. Also, the Organization will continue to provide the employee and his or her dependents with the same group insurance coverage.

Neither the Organization nor the insurance carrier will be liable for the payment of workers' compensation benefits for injuries that occur during an employee's voluntary participation in any off-duty recreational, social, or athletic activity sponsored by the Organization.

VACATION BENEFITS

Vacation time off with pay is available to eligible employees to provide opportunities for rest, relaxation, and personal pursuits. Employees in the following employment classifications are eligible to earn and use vacation time as described in this policy:

Regular full-time employees.
Regular part-time employees.

The amount of paid vacation time employees receive each year is shown in the following schedule. The schedule has been prepared based on a full-time workweek of five days per week and eight hours per day. A regular part-time employee's vacation schedule will be pro-rated by determining the ratio between time worked by the regular full-time employee compared to the regular part-time employee.

VACATION EARNING SCHEDULE

EMPLOYMENT CATEGORY	# OF WEEKS
Ministers and other exempt personnel	3
Nonexempt personnel	2

The length of eligible service is calculated on the basis of a "benefit year." This is the 12-month period that begins when the employee starts to earn vacation time. An employee's benefit year may be extended for any significant leave of absence except military leave of absence. Military leave has no effect on this calculation.

Once employees enter an eligible employment classification, they begin to earn paid vacation time according to the schedule. Earned vacation time is available for use in the year following its accrual.

All vacation time will be accrued on a calendar year basis. For those employees who begin work during a calendar year, vacation time will be accrued based on the schedule and time worked during the partial year. At January 1, vacation accrual will begin again for all employees.

Paid vacation time can be used in minimum increments of one-half day. To take vacation, employees should request advance approval from their supervisors. Requests will be reviewed based on a number of factors, including business needs and staffing requirements.

Vacation time off is paid at the employee's base pay rate at the time of vacation. It does not include overtime or any special forms of compensation such as incentives or bonuses.

All requests for vacation must be coordinated through the Administrator.

As stated above, employees are encouraged to use available paid vacation time for rest, relaxation, and personal pursuits. In the event that available vacation is not used by the end of the calendar year, December 31, employees will forfeit the unused time, unless prohibited by state law.

Upon termination of employment, employees will forfeit all unused vacation time that has been earned through the last day of work, unless prohibited by state law.

Resources

The following resources are recommended to the reader to assist them in the task of administration and planning.

Books by Dr. DeKoven

1. Leadership and Vision
2. Catch the Vision
3. Keys to Success
4. The Healing Community
5. Pastoral Leadership
6. How to Start a Ministry Training Center
7. Supernatural Architecture

Strategic Planning/Executive Coaching

Vision Leadership Institute - Dr. Stan DeKoven provides consulting to individuals in corporate or church environment, and to executive leadership.

Ministries

- Corporate Training, Motivational Speaking
- DISC Tools
- Counseling Center, Bible College Development for local church
- Policy & Procedures/Administrative helps
- Don Buckel, Administrative Assistance
- Ward Correll

For effective budgeting and financial management for churches or business, see *Budget Book Simplified* and *Christian Financial Business Management* by Dr. Roy DiFrancesca. Available through Vision Publishing.

About the Author

Dr. Stan DeKoven is a licensed Marriage, Family and Child counselor in California, and has worked for many years with clients suffering from the trauma of various losses. He is the founder and President of Vision International Education Network, with programs including Vision International University, Vision Publishing, Walk in Wisdom Ministries, and the Family Care Network, and is the author of over 30 books and study guides in practical Christian living for the maturing of God's people.

www.ingramcontent.com/pod-product-compliance
Lightning Source LLC
Chambersburg PA
CBHW031946080426
42735CB00007B/278